BETTER ANGELS: A PARABLE

*and*

EATING POMEGRANATES NAKED

# Better Angels: A Parable

*and*

# Eating Pomegranates Naked

Andrea Scott

*Better Angels: A Parable* and
*Eating Pomegranates Naked*
first published 2018 by Scirocco Drama
An imprint of J. Gordon Shillingford Publishing Inc.


Scirocco Drama Editor: Glenda MacFarlane

Cover design by Terry Gallagher/Doowah Design

Author photo by Tanja-Tiziana

Printed and bound in Canada on 100% post-consumer recycled paper.
We acknowledge the financial support of the Manitoba Arts Council and
The Canada Council for the Arts for our publishing program.



Production inquiries should be addressed to:
Playwright's Guild of Canada
401 Richmond Street West, Suite 350
Toronto, M5V 3A8
416-703-0201
www.playwrightsguild.ca

*Library and Archives Canada Cataloguing in Publication*

Scott, Andrea, 1971- (Playwright)
[Plays. Selections]
Better angels : a parable ; and, Eating pomegranates naked / Andrea Scott.

Two plays.
ISBN 978-1-927922-46-0 (softcover)

I. Scott, Andrea, 1971- (Playwright) . Better angels. II. Scott, Andrea, 1971- (Playwright) . Eating pomegranates naked. III. Title.

PS8637.C675A6 2018 C812'.6 C2018-904088-2

J. Gordon Shillingford Publishing
P.O. Box 86, RPO Corydon Avenue, Winnipeg, MB Canada R3M 3S3

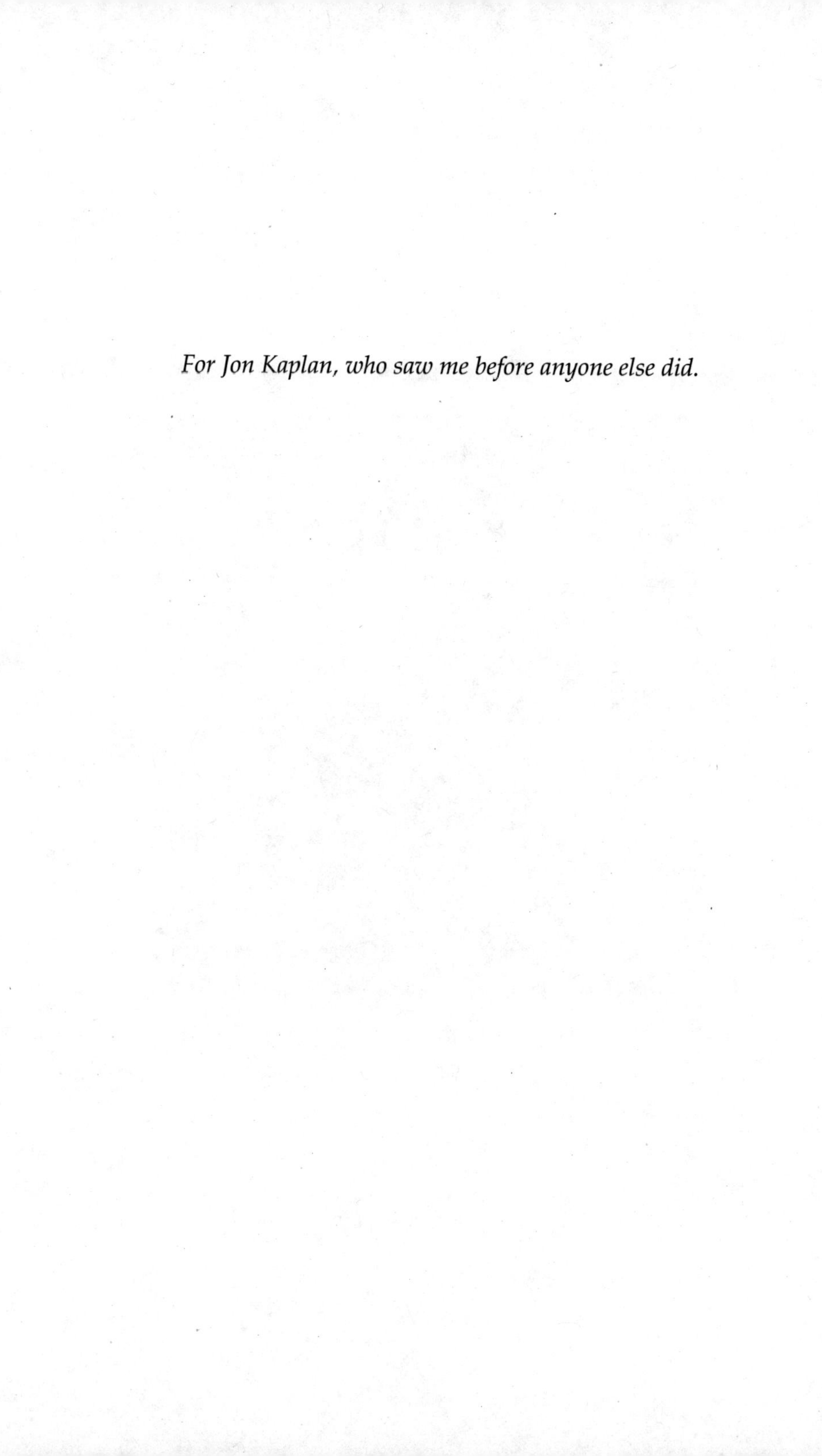

*For Jon Kaplan, who saw me before anyone else did.*

## Andrea Scott

Andrea Scott is a Toronto actor, playwright, and producer. Her first foray into writing was a one-woman show, *Damaged,* that debuted at bcurrent's rock.paper.sistahs festival in 2012. Her next play, *Eating Pomegranates Naked,* had staged readings at Alumnae Theatre, bcurrent, Obsidian Theatre, and Black Theatre Workshop, and won the RBC Arts Professional award at SummerWorks in 2013.

Two years later, *Better Angels: A Parable,* developed at Cahoots Theatre, won the SummerWorks award for Production and was recognized as Outstanding New Play, Outstanding Ensemble, Outstanding Direction, and Outstanding Production by *NOW Magazine.* It had its US debut at the Athena Festival in Chicago and was produced by Rumble Theatre in their Tremors Festival in 2016.

*Don't Talk to Me Like I'm Your Wife* won the Cayle Chernin Award for theatre in 2016, followed by a successful run at SummerWorks (Outstanding Performance – *NOW Magazine).* Andrea has also written plays for young audiences, including *Frenemies* for Mixed Company Theatre, and *Princesses Don't Grow on Trees* for Solar Stage Children's Theatre.

Andrea is a CAEA, ACTRA, PGC, DGA member and graduate from the Artist Producer Training Program run by Generator / Theatre Ontario. Andrea's new play, *Controlled Damage,* will be developed as part of bcurrent's 2018 / 2019 season.

# Acknowledgements

*Thanks to:* Fay Scott, Trevor Rock, Toronto Arts Council, Sylvia Neiman, Steven Neiman, Sheila Moll, Sarah Provo, Sara MacLean, Philip McKee, Sande Farrauto, Samantha Kaine, Sabryn Rock, Roni Hoffman, Rong Fu, Rumble Theatre, Robert Watson, Philip Akin, Phanom Chanthavong, Paulette Mazenc, Paul Robinson, SummerWorks Festival, Ontario Arts Council, Obsidian Theatre, Ontario Arts Council, Nova Printing, Nina Lee Aquino, Nancy Carr, Nana Aba Duncan, Myrtle Ashman, Mary-Lynn Smith, Milkface Nursingware, Mike and Maria Mallinos, Michael Reid, Nancy Copeland, Mel Hague, Mark Michaud, Marjorie Chan, Margaret Schulzke, Andrea Seymore, Michael Rubenfeld, Meghan Swaby, *NOW Magazine*, Lyndsay Thibault, Lucid Fitness, Leslie Thomson, Leah-Simone Bowen, Leo Dyer Insurance, LemonTree Creations, Laura Scott, Kimberly Radmacher, Kerr Bros Ltd., Norah Cuzzocrea, Keriece Harris, Rosa LaBordé, Katie Lumsden, Idle Muse Theatre Company, Joanna Falck, Julie Florio, Joseph Jomo Pierre, Jiv Parasram, Jennifer Green, Janet and Roger Beck, Hilary June Hart, Garfield Portch, Factory Theatre, Esther Jun, Erin Birkenbergs, Expect Theatre, Eileen Li, Dinah Watts, Derek Barber, Dayan Scott, Dawn Morgan, David Moase, David and Robin Craig, Daniel de Pas, Dairy Farmers of Canada, Deb Smyth, Dahlia Katz, Colin Doyle, Cole Alvis, Cobs Bakery, Conor Green, Cherissa Richards, Chapman's Ice Cream, Canada Council, Cahoots Theatre, b current Theatre, Black Theatre Workshop, Britt Lennox, Bridget Ogundipe, Black Theatre Workshop, Tarragon Theatre, Barbara Fingerote, Andrew Lamb, Alumnae Theatre, Alison and Arvind Sharma, Alex Zarowny, Annemieke Wade, the Vincent Graves Greene Foundation for Philatelic Research, Pat Bradley, and David Christo.

# Playwright's Notes

The first play I ever read featuring brown and black women was *for colored girls who have considered suicide/when the rainbow is enuf* by Ntozake Shange. It has remained my guide in creating voices for the stage that are loud, lyrical, loving, and truthful.

Black women on stage are rare; black women with agency and the ability to save themselves are rarer still. In *Better Angels: A Parable,* Akosua uses her intelligence, wit, and notes cribbed from Anansi, the West African spider god.

*Eating Pomegranates Naked* was inspired by a murmuration of starlings in the skies above me and their chattering as they landed in a gorgeous swoop. To me they were like women working together, talking over one another, but still a supportive infrastructure. That is how Sera the swan, Anaar the peacock, and Cassidy the grackle were born.

In both plays the women feel imprisoned by their bodies, their fears, and entrenched societal expectations – and words are the keys to set them free. Thank you for joining them on their journey.

# BETTER ANGELS

*A Parable*

"We are not enemies, but friends.
We must not be enemies. Though
passion may have strained, it must not
break our bonds of affection. The mystic
chords of memory will swell when
again touched, as surely they will be,
by the better angels of our nature."

– Abraham Lincoln

"Vengeance comes from the individual
and punishment from God."

– Victor Hugo

## Production History

*Better Angels: A Parable* debuted at the SummerWorks Performance Festival in Toronto, Ontario in August of 2015 with the following team:

AKOSUA Mansa ......... Akosua Amo-Adem
LEILA Tate .................................. Sascha Cole
GREG Tate.................................. Peyson Rock
911 DISPATCHER...................... Andrea Scott

Director: Nigel Shawn Williams
Set and Costume Design: Laura Gardner
Sound Design: Verne Good
Lighting Design: Jennifer Lennon
Stage Manager: Farnoosh Talebpour
Dramaturge: Marjorie Chan
Producer: Call Me Scotty Productions

*Winner of the 2015 SummerWorks Prize for Outstanding Production.*

Akosua (Akosua Amo-Adem) describes freedom.
*Photo by Dahlia Katz.*

Greg (Peyson Rock) and Leila Tate (Sascha Cole) show Akosua (Akosua Amo-Adem) her room.
*Photo by Dahlia Katz.*

Your husband is not who you think he is. Leila (Sascha Cole) and Greg (Peyson Rock).
*Photo by Dahlia Katz.*

Greg (Peyson Rock) considers what he's done.
*Photo by Dahlia Katz.*

## Characters

LEILA Tate:
a woman in her early 30s (any ethnicity).

AKOSUA Mansa:
an African woman from Ghana in her 20s.

GREG Tate:
LEILA's husband in his early 30s,
he is a light-skinned black man.

# Prologue

*Dark stage. Projected on the screen is the transcript of the 911 call. This can be projected in silence or a recording can be played.*

DISPATCHER: 911. What is your emergency?

WITNESS: Yeah, uh, I think something bad has happened at my neighbours' house.

DISPATCHER: Where are you located?

WITNESS: What did you say?

DISPATCHER: Where are you located? Where is the emergency?

WITNESS: Crawford Park Hills.

DISPATCHER: Can I get an exact address, please?

WITNESS: *(Bleeped.)* Street. On the east side of the street across from the big tree that was cut down after the ice storm.

DISPATCHER: What is the emergency?

WITNESS: It looks like something bad has happened at the Tate house. I mean, something violent.

DISPATCHER: Violent?

WITNESS: Yeah. I mean, I was walking by, you know, walking my dog and I noticed, I saw the door, their door, the Tates? That's their name. I noticed that their door was open. Claymore, my dog, was freaking out and trying to get to the door so I went up there, you know, onto the front steps and that's when I saw the blood.

DISPATCHER: Blood, ma'am?

WITNESS: Yes, there was blood, on the inside of the front hallway and I could see bodies.

DISPATCHER: Bodies?

WITNESS: There were bodies…I think they're dead. I think my neighbours are dead.

DISPATCHER: Please don't go into the house, ma'am. The police are on their way. What is your name, ma'am?

WITNESS: Nancy.

DISPATCHER: Can I get a last name? (*Dial tone.)*

*End of call.*

## Scene 1

*The stage is dark and AKOSUA is standing in a pool of light. She smiles easily and speaks in a slight Ghanaian accent. There is a piece of luggage at her feet.*

AKOSUA: There is nothing like the feeling of flying. In my dreams I used to fly all the time. Of course when I woke up I knew I could not fly. I was so sad I would sit and look out the window and dream. My parents said that dreams were wonderful but that is why we could not stay in them forever. Then on my seventh birthday they gave me a bicycle. It was the most beautiful thing in the world to me. It had a FanMilk sticker on the back and a red bell on the front. When I would ride my bike I felt like I was really flying. Have you ever gotten on a bike and just felt free? You can go anywhere, see everything and feel the wind on your face. The sun warms your shoulders and gets into your eyes but you don't care because you are smiling so, so wide. That is what it means to be free. Then, someone stole my bicycle. It was gone for maybe two weeks when I saw a big, fat boy ride past our house on it. I grabbed my parents and we looked for this boy. When we found him he was sitting on his small, front porch eating an apple. "You stole my bike!" I yelled at him. His eyes got really big and he said, "My da gave this bike to me. You are calling him a thief," and he stormed into the house. When he returned he had his father and mother with him. The father said, "I bought this bike for my boy. How dare you call him a liar. Besides, you cannot prove that it is yours." I looked at my mommy and daddy and they asked me if I was sure it was mine and I said yes. But the more they questioned me the more I became unsure. But then as we were walking away I noticed the FanMilk sticker on the back and I said, "There! That proves that it is mine.

Give it back!" And the father of the boy said, "That proves nothing. Give us a picture of you on this bike and we will return it. You cannot prove it because it is not yours. Besides, if you did not lock it up then you don't deserve it." And with that they walked into the house and took the bike away. That was the first time that I realized that life is not fair and we must guard it very carefully. My parents could not afford another bike so I never got to have that flying feeling again. That is the thing about freedom: You do not know how it feels until it is taken from you and then you will do anything to get it back.

## Scene 2

*One year ago.*

*We are in GREG and LEILA's living room. It is in disarray but spacious. AKOSUA is wearing a simple outfit and carrying two pieces of luggage. LEILA is a dark-haired stylish woman who always wears black; she is warm, helpful, and all smiles. GREG is well-dressed, quiet, and watchful. The couple watches AKOSUA as she gets acclimatized to the space, looking around and picking up photos.*

AKOSUA: Your children are beautiful.

GREG: Thank you. They're great. They've been at camp for about…how long has it been, honey?

LEILA: Oh wow, I'd say, mmm, coming on two weeks now. They'll be back in a couple of days.

AKOSUA: Oh, so they're not here?

LEILA: No, sorry. You'll get lots of time with them when they get back and then you'll be looking forward to when they start school again.

GREG: They're not that bad.

LEILA: No, no, no! I just meant the noise, sometimes.

AKOSUA: *(Picking up a picture of GREG and LEILA.)* This is sweet. How old were you here?

LEILA: *(Taking the photo and thinking.)* Oh gosh! I never look at these pictures, you know? They're on the mantel and they just become part of the wallpaper.

GREG: I think we were like, eighteen? Maybe a little older.

AKOSUA: How did you meet?

GREG: *(Taking the photo from LEILA but staying close to her.)* Ahhh!

LEILA: *(Laughing.)* It's really cheesy.

GREG: Come on!

LEILA: *(Smiling.)* We were both at this, like, this poetry thingie and this hippie-dippie girl gets up on stage and she's full on flower power. I mean, long skirt, hair down to here, John Lennon glasses and, well, you know, the full nine yards –

GREG: Leila and I didn't know each other then but we were sitting at the same table.

LEILA: BUT –

GREG: But then she started speaking –

LEILA: "You held out the light, You held out the light –

*GREG joins in.*

LEILA & GREG: To light my cigarette. But when I leaned down to the flame it singed my eyebrows and hair – "

GREG: My favourite Gwendolyn MacEwen poem. Ever.

LEILA: Our favourite. How does it end again?

GREG: Uh…mmm…can't remember. Weird.

LEILA: We were both big smokers then. So, we bonded over mocking the incense girl, then the poem and then we went for a smoke.

GREG: But we don't smoke anymore.

LEILA: Oh no! Cut that out when the kids came. Now our biggest vices are tea and *The Amazing Race.* I don't know about you but I could really use a cup of tea. Greg?

GREG: Earl Grey, mint, lapsang souchong…?

LEILA: Surprise me. Aggie, would you like some tea?

*AKOSUA does not respond as she is looking around the room – and also, LEILA is calling her by the incorrect name.*

Aggie…

*LEILA taps AKOSUA on the shoulder.*

AKOSUA: Oh!

LEILA: Tea?

AKOSUA: Yes, yes thank you, yes. That would be nice.

LEILA: And Greg?

*GREG is looking at his phone.*

Greg?

GREG: Mm…yeah?

LEILA: Sweetie, could you bring some of those cookies from the top shelf? Thanks.

*GREG exits. Once he gets into the kitchen he begins texting while throwing looks over his shoulder furtively.*

Sometimes he can be so… *(Mimes strangling someone.)* So…sit down, relax. This has probably been the longest day in your life.

AKOSUA: It's exciting.

LEILA: I'm sure. Have you ever been on a plane before?

AKOSUA: No, I was so scared.

LEILA: Of what?

AKOSUA: That it would crash.

LEILA: Thousands of planes take off every day in the world and we hear about planes crashing once or twice a year. I'm sure there are hundreds of flights from Africa to Canada and I can't remember if there's ever been an accident. And what are the chances that your first time on a plane is your final voyage? Tiny!

AKOSUA: I suppose you're right. It was so strange how it felt when the plane started to move. It didn't feel like flying at all. I was holding on so tight that I didn't even want to go to the washroom.

LEILA: But you did, right?

AKOSUA: Hm?

LEILA: The bathroom…you didn't hold it, did you?

AKOSUA: Oh no.

LEILA: Good. I'd hate to have to take you to the doctor because you got a bladder infection.

AKOSUA: I was sitting beside a very nice lady and she told me it would be okay. I must have looked the fool walking very slowly to the washroom afraid that I would fall out of the plane. I always thought flying would feel different.

LEILA: Yes, well, you have your feet firmly on the ground and you're safe.

AKOSUA: Al Hamdu-Lillah.

LEILA: I'm sorry. What did you say? (*GREG enters with a tray.*)

AKOSUA: Would you like some help?

GREG: Oh no. Thank you. Today is your day off *(Laughs.)* so just sit tight. You didn't say how you like your tea so I left it black.

AKOSUA: Sweet and very milky. *(She begins to eat the cookies greedily.)*

GREG: Well, we don't keep sugar in the house except Splenda and we only use soy milk. I hope that's okay.

LEILA: Were you speaking a different language?

AKOSUA: It's Arabic. It means "Praise be to God."

LEILA: Oh.

AKOSUA: I'm Muslim.

LEILA: Ahhh.

AKOSUA: Islam is practised in different parts of Africa.

LEILA: You know, I did know that but completely forgot. Greg's Jewish.

GREG: Lapsed, actually. I don't go to temple or –

LEILA: I don't think there are any temples or mosques for you to pray at in this neighbourhood.

AKOSUA: Thank you, but I will be fine. The tea is lovely.

LEILA: From now on that is your cup and plate.

AKOSUA: My cup and plate?

LEILA: Yes, yours. Keep them in your room if you like.

AKOSUA: Oh…thank you. *(Looking around the room.)* You have a lovely home; what do you do for a living, Mrs. Tate?

LEILA: Please call me Leila. And I'm a writer.

AKOSUA: Oh. So, you don't work.

LEILA: I'm working on a novel.

GREG: Well, she hasn't made any money from it yet. She's one step away from being a poet!

LEILA: Greg!

GREG: Kidding! Seriously though, she's really good.

*As LEILA is speaking, GREG reaches up and pulls her hair out of a soft ponytail.*

LEILA: If I could just publish one thing! Greg is so supportive. I quit my normal job to focus on this dream to be a writer. Greg!

*She grabs his hand and kisses it.*

GREG: She's so pretty with her hair down, don't you think?

LEILA: *(Fixedly looks at GREG.)* She hardly knows me. *(Turns back, with softer tone.)* You hardly know me but we have lots of time for us to get to know one another; let's give you a tour.

GREG: I'll be right back. I just got a text from work. *(Holds up phone.)* I swear if I'm not getting it from the General here they're cracking the whip at the office.

*GREG makes the cracking the whip sound/ gesture. He moves to the shadows, where we can see him smiling and texting.*

LEILA: He has no idea how hard it is, you know? Writing? I mean, there's nothing worse than staring at a blank page and having no idea what to write next. I'd rather be doing your job! Not that scrubbing toilets isn't work, but it's not mentally difficult like coming up with stories, right?

AKOSUA: Mmm. Only a stupid person would have problems writing a story, yes?

LEILA: I'm not sure that's what I meant…

AKOSUA: Just put one word after another.

LEILA: Right…wise words. Is that an African saying?

AKOSUA: Neil Gaiman said it.

LEILA: Who?

AKOSUA: Just a writer I enjoy.

LEILA: *(Nodding.)* ….Oh! So I don't forget, can I get your passport? I have a safe place to keep it and I need it to fill out some forms about your job with us. My kids can sometimes get into mischief and if they get a hold of your passport you'll never find it. Don't worry, you'll get it back.

*AKOSUA hands the passport to her. LEILA flips it open, looks at it for a moment and tucks it into her purse.*

Nice picture. We all look like criminals in our passport pictures.

AKOSUA: Your kids are five and seven, yes?

*GREG enters without the phone.*

LEILA: Close. Maggie is seven and Christopher is nine. They will wear you out, but I'm sure you can handle it. It will be like having a big sister around.

AKOSUA: I was the smallest in my family, so it will be nice to be the eldest for once.

GREG: You're going to be a part of this family in no time.

*They all move to another part of the stage that until this point has been in darkness. Once the lights come up it will reveal a lovely, girly bedroom. LEILA has gone all out. There's even a tiny flag of Ghana on the bedside table.*

LEILA: Now I know it doesn't look like much, and Greg and I were planning to get you a TV and radio, but we just ran out of time. You understand. Besides, I'm sure it's better than what you had back home, right? Feel free to put up pictures and stuff. I have double-sided tape that won't mess up the paint job.

GREG: It was either this or the basement, which is cool in the summer but it's kinda creepy down there with cobwebs and spiders. Besides, when you're here you're closer to us and the kids. Win-Win!

LEILA: The bathroom is just down the hall if you want to freshen up before bed. I like an early start to my day, so I'm probably gonna need you to be up no later than 7:00. The alarm clock is there, but if I don't see you in the kitchen tomorrow morning I'm going to be waking you up.

AKOSUA: I'll be there.

GREG: She's not kidding! I've been on the receiving end of a cold cup of water in the midst of a deep slumber, believe you me!

AKOSUA: I wake up early.

LEILA: Good! See you in the morning, and welcome to the family!

*GREG and LEILA exit with the sound effect of a door slamming shut, leaving us alone with AKOSUA. The room is illuminated with a dim overhead light and she inspects her narrow room and notices a spider in a web in the down-stage corner of her "room."*

AKOSUA: Hello, friend.

## Scene 3

*LEILA and GREG in their room as they get ready for bed. There is still a dim light on AKOSUA in her room so we can see what she is doing while their scene is happening. She is unpacking her suitcase and removes a prayer rug. She will be performing the "isha" prayer as the scene proceeds.*

LEILA: Not bad, huh?

GREG: Yeah, she seems pretty nice.

LEILA: Mmm, well, I hope the religion thing doesn't get in the way.

GREG: Get in the way? Why would it?

LEILA: I don't know. Maybe she'll refuse to do something because it's against her religion.

GREG: Leila, she's here to take care of the house and kids, don't be ignorant.

LEILA: I'm not being ignorant, but you know a person can justify their actions using religion as a reason.

GREG: Don't start.

LEILA: Don't start what?

GREG: You know. And what was that crack about being Jewish?

LEILA: You're being over-sensitive, it wasn't a crack, it was a-a-a, I dunno, a way to make her feel comfortable about being a Muslim.

GREG: By saying I'm a Jew?

LEILA: So she knows that religion isn't a foreign concept in this house.

GREG: It's not?

LEILA: We got married in a church, didn't we?

GREG: So!

LEILA: So there are pictures all over the house of us in the church, outside the church. We're not against God.

GREG: Not against God?? What are you talking about? We haven't been in a church since we got married.

LEILA: Does that bother you?

GREG: I'm Jewish, I don't care.

LEILA: Well, you're not really Jewish. I mean, you are but…

GREG: Leila…

LEILA: I wonder what your mother would think of us hiring a black Muslim housekeeper.

GREG: My mom barely see us. I'm sure she wouldn't care.

LEILA: She'd think it was in keeping with the crazy choices you've always made. Marrying a goyim –

GREG: Stop using words you don't understand.

LEILA: Okay…uh…marrying a shiksa, giving up Judaism, having non-Jewish kids…hiring a black AND Muslim housekeeper. What's next?

GREG: *(Big sigh.)* I'm going to bed.

LEILA: Okay, fine. I'm sorry.

GREG: For what?

LEILA: Nothing. I guess I'm a little wound up, having a stranger in the house.

GREG: You wanted live-in help around the house and now you have it. Besides, she won't be a stranger forever.

LEILA: Right…right…I just hope…. Having a domestic in the house doesn't make me a bad person. You don't leave your home thousands of miles away because you're happy. That girl came here for work and now she has a place to live, food to eat, and a job. A lot of Canadian citizens don't have that. She's lucky to be with us.

GREG: You're so sexy when you ramble. Wanna fool around? *(Slips his hand under LEILA's shirt.)*

LEILA: You're not listening to me.

GREG: Yes, I am. You're worried she won't like you and –

LEILA: I didn't say that.

GREG: *(Pause.)* So, you don't want to fool around?

LEILA: –

GREG: The house is all ours…no kids.

LEILA: What's got into you? *(Giggles.)*

GREG: Come 'ere!

## Scene 4

*The kitchen the next morning. LEILA is instructing AKOSUA.*

LEILA: So, my kids compete over everything because that's what kids do. I used to make them special lunches, you know, with something different for each kid. You know, applesauce for one, pudding for the other, and ham and cheese on a bagel for one, tuna for the other, well, you get the idea. Anyway, I found out from the school that they were sharing one lunch between the two of them because they didn't like getting different things. They wanted the same thing! Isn't that weird? When I was a kid I hated getting the same thing as my brother. I loved opening my lunch box – it was a Mickey Mouse lunchbox that my parents bought me when they went to Disney World – and seeing what I got this time. Sometimes my treat would be a Mickey's Banana Flip or a Twinkie or even a bag of chips. I can't imagine giving my kids chips for a school snack now. Oh yeah, and no matter how much they whine, never give them foods containing sugar, a lot of salt, or fat.

AKOSUA: What about the pudding? Isn't that sugar?

LEILA: Ah, Well, here is the magic of living in the First World. (*Reaches under the counter to pull out the container.*) ZenSoy pudding! No dairy and it comes in vanilla, chocolate and, my favourite, vanilla / chocolate swirl. I'll bet you've never seen that in your village. *(She opens one and starts eating it.)* I know it's early but a little cheating never hurt anyone, right? Our little secret.

AKOSUA: Yes…so when I wake up I am to make the coffee –

LEILA: And that is…where?

AKOSUA: You keep it…here.

LEILA: Right, go on.

AKOSUA: So, I make the coffee, empty the dishwasher, make the kids their lunch –

LEILA: No. Wake the kids first, then the coffee; then make their breakfast followed by lunch. If you start doing work around the kitchen, time will get away from you and then the kids are up late and the lunches aren't made. You have all morning to empty the dishwasher.

AKOSUA: Okay, I'm sorry.

LEILA: Again.

AKOSUA: Make the coffee, wake the kids, start making their breakfast –

LEILA: And what do they like?

AKOSUA: Cereal and yogurt for Maggie and toast with peanut butter for Christopher.

LEILA: And one banana sliced up for both of them. Maggie likes to mush it up in her cereal and Chris likes it sliced on top of his peanut butter. Make sure the banana is soft enough to squish but hard enough to slice.

AKOSUA: Okay.

LEILA: Well, colour me surprised! It sounds like you have the morning with the kids pretty much down. Make sure they have their lunches in their backpacks. I don't want to have to go down to the school at lunchtime. I just hate the smell of elementary schools, especially at lunch. Just thinking about it I can smell the egg salad and warm tuna on Wonder Bread. (*Fake retches and laughs.*)

AKOSUA: If they do forget their lunch, should I go down to the school with it?

LEILA: Oh no. I'll drive down. No need to interrupt your day. I mean, it is an inconvenience, since I'm trying to finish writing my book and these stupid distractions always happen at the worst possible time. Do you know how to drive?

AKOSUA: No.

LEILA: Good, then I guess I don't have to worry about getting you insured. I should take you for a drive in the city. Toronto is really pretty, if you're in the right neighbourhood. All you got to see last night were the lights, and while it's nice at night, you need to see it in the daytime.

AKOSUA: Maybe I can go for a walk, since the children aren't back yet.

LEILA: Hmm…Toronto may seem really safe, but it's dangerous when you're new to the city. There are shootings.

AKOSUA: Shootings?

LEILA: Mmhmm… in malls, at barbeques, even on the streets when you're just trying to do your shopping. I would never forgive myself if anything happened to you.

AKOSUA: I thought Canada was safer than the United States.

LEILA: In some ways, yes, but this is a big city and you're a young girl. It would be like throwing you to the sharks if you left the house without me. Unless you have friends in Toronto, do you?

AKOSUA: Here?

LEILA: Friends, you don't have any friends in the city, right?

AKOSUA: No, nobody.

LEILA: What am I saying? *We're* your new friends and family. Besides, don't worry, we'll send you home for Christmas. I know you don't celebrate it but Greg and I will be home and the kids will be off school, so why not give you a break so you can see your family back home.

AKOSUA: That is very kind of you, Mrs. Tate.

LEILA: Please call me Leila. Now will you be a dear and take this into my study? I can't function without a cup of coffee when I'm writing.

AKOSUA: Yes, Mrs. Tate.

*As she's about to exit, LEILA continues speaking.*

LEILA: This has been a great first day... I mean, the last girl we hired had an ECE degree and was useless. She was forgetful, couldn't follow simple instructions and gave me attitude over breaks and – Oh! And she smoked. She didn't think I knew, but I saw her once when she was off the clock. I just said to Greg, nope, we're not doing this. Bad influence on the kids and kind of a temptation for two ex-smokers, you know?

AKOSUA: She lived here?

LEILA: No, she had her own place, and that was a nightmare, because she started getting here later and later. I know, from having a job that I hated, that when you start showing up late, it's because you hate your job. And I totally understand hating your job but she was young and hadn't worked much. But she started talking about labour laws, and I can't do that, and you can't tell me to do this, you know? It so easy to talk about the laws and what's right and wrong but at least do the fricken job, right? She was easy to fire.

AKOSUA: Oh.

LEILA: Don't worry, you're already way better than she was after six months. I'm just so happy you're here. *(Puts her arm around AKOSUA.)* You know, I helped build a school in Ghana.

AKOSUA: Really?

LEILA: Mmhmm. As a teenager. I love Africa and the people. So giving and kind. It's the reason Greg and I decided on Ghana over the Philippines like all the other people in our neighbourhood. You're from the capital, right?

AKOSUA: Yes, Accra. Hot, sticky, loud in the city, but on the coast, where I lived, it is cool enough for a sweater. So many places that would take your breath away. We also have castles.

LEILA: Castles?

AKOSUA: Yes. There are shacks and tall office buildings and loud traffic but there are also many castles. They were built by the Dutch, the Portuguese, and the British hundreds of years ago. The slave trade was very active in Ghana and those big buildings are a reminder of the past, which was not so long ago.

LEILA: *(Almost to herself.)* Castles in Accra…that would make a great title.

AKOSUA: Title?

LEILA: For a novel or even a chapter. It just scans beautifully. And the image of a beautiful castle in Africa, kind of a fish out of water, you know? And the fact that it was there because of slavery…I think I'm going to use that, do you mind?

AKOSUA: No, Mrs. Tate.

LEILA: Call me Leila, please.

AKOSUA: Yes, Leila.

LEILA: Did you fantasize about being a princess and being swept away into one of those castles?

AKOSUA: *(Bluntly.)* No.

LEILA: Huh. I thought all little girls wanted to be princesses and live in a castle.

*AKOSUA smiles and says nothing.*

Oh! And remind me that we have to sit down and talk about compensation. I meant to talk about to you about it last night but we were all so tired.

AKOSUA: We could talk about it now.

LEILA: True…that is true, but as Zadie Smith says, "it's important for a writer to be protective of her writing time," and I've eaten into that chatting with you. Let's sit down and talk about it on your break, but first let me show you the kids' rooms. I tidied them a bit but, as you can see, housekeeping isn't my strength. You are a godsend. And I love that your English is impeccable. Does everyone in Ghana speak English this well? *(They exit the room.)*

## Scene 5

*Later that evening. GREG and LEILA getting ready for bed while AKOSUA is doing her evening prayers in dim light.*

GREG: So, how was the first day?

LEILA: Fine. She's a quick study. I don't think we'll have a problem with her.

GREG: The place looks great. I barely recognized it, it was so clean.

LEILA: Thanks! *(She punches him in the arm playfully.)*

GREG: What?

LEILA: Greg, this girl is way better than any maid service. She started cleaning after breakfast and didn't stop until 10:30 tonight.

GREG: Did she take a break?

LEILA: Of course. That reminds me…I was supposed to talk to her about payment…. I gave her some lunch around 3:00 and was about to talk to her about it when I came up with a great sentence and had to write it down. Anyways, she's awesome. This isn't like some privileged white girl throwing around rules and labour law bullshit. She works like a mule and doesn't complain.

GREG: Yeah, well, keep an eye on her. She may not complain but she might steal shit in order to feel compensated.

LEILA: For what? We brought her here and we're giving her free room and board. This is Canada, not some Third World country without toilets and electricity. She's grateful. I've never seen anyone work so hard.

GREG: Just be careful. I don't want any of our stuff ending up in a pawn shop.

LEILA: That would require her leaving and she's never going to leave the house.

GREG: Don't be so sure.

LEILA: No, Greg, you don't understand, she's afraid to leave the house. I told her how dangerous it is out there.

GREG: *(Using air quotes.)* Out there?

LEILA: How is she going to know the difference between our neighbourhood and, say, any ghetto area in the city?

GREG: Please don't use the word *ghetto* –

LEILA: Yeah yeah, but listen, if she's too scared to leave the house we have nothing to worry about. I showed her some stories about people being dismembered and left in suitcases, proof of police brutality and all the shootings we've had.

GREG: All the shootings we've had? You mean all four?

LEILA: If all I show her is the violence in Toronto, that's all she'll know. It's not like she can look it up on the internet.

GREG: What do we do if she gets sick?

LEILA: We can worry about that when it happens. Until then let's celebrate that we have a housekeeper, a nanny, a clean house, and no kids for two days all rolled into one. *(She kisses him.)*

GREG: *(He resists.)* Yeah, that's great. You know, I'm really tired and I have to go in a little earlier tomorrow. Raincheck? *(He rolls over to go to sleep.)*

LEILA: Uh…yeah…sure. The office wife is really cracking the whip, isn't she?

GREG: Office wife?

LEILA: Janice. Calling you at home. Late. Working you like a dog at the office.

GREG: She's not my office wife, she's my boss.

LEILA: She sees you more than I do.

GREG: *(Sits up.)* I am really, really not up for this tonight. I have told you that Janice is my co-worker. My superior, really. Sometimes I get called at home. Sometimes I have to work late. I don't like it, but it's what I have to do. We are living on one salary now.

LEILA: Don't try to make me feel guilty.

GREG: I'm not trying to make you feel guilty. I'm happy you get to do what you want, but that does mean I'm a little less free with my time now, you know? September is going to be crazy. Janice is away at her cottage with her kids for the long weekend, so I'm on deck. Full stop. *(Pause.)* Do you need me to say it?

LEILA: No.

GREG: I love you, Ley. I am not having an affair with Janice. She is not my office wife.

LEILA: You didn't have to say that. *(She's pleased.)*

GREG: Getting help in the house was the best idea for the family. For us.

LEILA: She gave me the best idea today, without really meaning to.

GREG: *(Lying back down.)* Uh huh? Something for the book?

LEILA: Yea, she told me that Accra has castles. Did you know that?

GREG: Nope. Africans built castles?

LEILA: No. Well, yes, kind of. The colonialists moved in, decided to build castles and used the people that lived there as free labour.

GREG: Gotta love the English. That's great, Ley. I know you were feeling stuck.

LEILA: It wasn't just the Brits. It was the Dutch, the Portuguese, even the Swedes. I think I have my hook. A slave that falls in love with the slave trader and he puts her up in the castle…or no… He falls for her, yes. He sees her in the chains and her helplessness and beauty make him want to rescue her from being sold to a cruel land owner in Jamaica or something. Hmm…it will have a historical fiction bent with the poetry of the lands around them. Oh, yes…this – I can't wait to –

*LEILA notices that GREG is asleep. She sits up, staring ahead for a moment, then gets out of bed, walks over to AKOSUA's room and locks the door. AKOSUA sits up at the sound but eventually lies back down.*

## Scene 6

*Two months have passed and we're closing in on Christmas. LEILA has her coat on and car keys in her hand. GREG is in the study at the computer playing Candy Crush or whatever addictive video game is current (we can hear the sound effects). AKOSUA is in her room with headphones on. At some point she will remove them, leave her room, and overhear GREG's conversation.*

LEILA: I'm leaving now. We're going to try and make this a short shopping trip, but parking is such a bitch, it may take more than a couple of hours.

GREG: Language, Leila!

LEILA: The kids are in the car, your highness! Anyway, see you in a few hours.

GREG: Bye!

*He waits a bit before checking to see that she's really gone, then pulls out a bag of Halloween candy and makes a call on his cell.*

Hey.

HIM: Hi.

GREG: I'm putting you on speaker.

HIM: You're alone, I take it.

GREG: Sort of. Ley and the kids are at the mall. What are you doing?

HIM: I'm at the office.

GREG: It's Saturday.

HIM: I know. I have to catch up on a few things and it's so quiet here on the weekend. Janice is killing me with these reports and I don't want to take them home with me. That's our special place and I don't want it polluted with her negative chi....Hello?

GREG: Sorry.

HIM: Are you playing that stupid game?

GREG: I'm sorry. I was listening…negative chi, Janice is a bitch.

HIM: That's not what I said.

GREG: Let's start over. I've closed the game.

HIM: I don't know if this is working.

GREG: What? What are you working on? Maybe I can log on remotely and help.

HIM: No. I mean, us.

GREG: What are you talking about? We're fine.

HIM: You're married, Greg. I am gay. We're…what are we? A couple? A couple only when we sneak off on breaks or on business trips? I feel like a dirty little secret and I promised myself I would never ever do that to myself again.

GREG: Baby, please don't do this to me. Not now. *(Takes HIM off speaker phone.)* ….I'm confused. Tell my… Tell her what? That I'm gay and in love with my account director…? You have no fucking idea. Seriously. Do you know how much I would lose if I told Leila that I'm gay? Can you even imagine? Everything. Every goddamn thing. And I am not letting my kids go. Nothing will come between me and my kids. If she found out she would… I think she'd actually kill me, but it's not her I'm worried about, since she'll be fine. She's still really attractive and…she could find someone. No, it's my kids I can't live without. She knows that and would keep me from them just to punish me. You are not breaking up with me over the phone. Come on! Listen, my wife thinks I'm fucking Janice. I know, right? She hasn't got a clue about us. Let's take a trip. I'll tell Leila that I have a conference to attend in, uh...somewhere crappy that she won't want to go and we'll get some time together. I'm going online right now to look for packages. You like a window seat, right? Don't worry about Leila, I'll take care of her. John, hun, we'll be just fine.

*AKOSUA tiptoes to her room and smiles.*

## Scene 7

*LEILA is sitting in front of her laptop in her study and she's frustrated. The calendar shows that it is now November and there is a bag of Rockets candy beside the laptop. AKOSUA is dusting the room. LEILA is eating the Rockets. She begins watching AKOSUA.*

LEILA: Do you celebrate Halloween? I mean, where you're from?

AKOSUA: Well, no, but it is celebrated in some parts of Africa. Any reason to throw a jol.

LEILA: I'm sorry, a what?

AKOSUA: Sorry, a party. People love to celebrate and have fun. Dress up, act the fool.

LEILA: Huh. Yeah, well, I got married on Halloween. I definitely acted the fool on that day.

AKOSUA: Did you dress up?

LEILA: We made it a costume wedding but not crazy, you know? People could wear something nice but a cool mask.

AKOSUA: Sounds fun.

LEILA: I couldn't drink, so it was fun for Greg, not so much for me.

*At AKOSUA's quizzical look, LEILA indicates that she was pregnant.*

AKOSUA: Ohhh.

LEILA: Yea. I had all these dreams and then I met Greg and we both loved poetry and literature and just being free, you know?

AKOSUA: I do.

LEILA: You have a boyfriend back home?

AKOSUA: Oh no, nothing serious.

LEILA: Good. Wait. Enjoy your life. Nobody tells you how hard marriage is going to be. It's like marrieds keep quiet until the door slams shut and then they all huddle around and say, "Seeeeee, it's a fucking shell game!" *(Giggles ruefully.)* Are your parents still married?

AKOSUA: Oh yes. Forty-five years. Very happy.

LEILA: Don't get me wrong. I like being married, but nobody tells you that sometimes you feel lonely in a marriage. You know what I mean? I look at him, Greg, while he's sleeping and I think, "I love you but I don't really know you." I mean, now that I'm married I can't try new things.

AKOSUA: Like what?

LEILA: Well, I'll never be with a woman.

AKOSUA: Oh! *(Pause.)* Do you want to?

LEILA: Not right now, of course, but who knows… maybe someday. And I never slept with a black guy, not once.

AKOSUA: But your husband is…

LEILA: I mean like a really black man, "Idris Elba" black, you know? And I've been to Africa, so I totally could have. Hey, what's that? *(Gesturing to the bracelet on AKOSUA's wrist.)*

AKOSUA: What? Oh, this? Magpie gave it to me.

LEILA: Magpie? Who's Magpie?

AKOSUA: Sorry. Maggie.

LEILA: *(Stops eating and blanches a little.)* My Maggie?

AKOSUA: Yes. I call her Magpie because she's always scrounging for this and that to make things. It's a friendship bracelet she made for me using the colours of my flag by adding little star trinkets to it. She is so sweet and funny. Creative, too.

LEILA: Mmm, yes, I know. She's my child.

AKOSUA: Okay.

*There is a long, awkward pause.*

LEILA: I can't believe I quit my job to be a writer when I can't get past this chapter. I might as well get a job writing pamphlets for Health Canada… Speaking of, did Chris ever pass that marble?

AKOSUA: Yes.

LEILA: I swear, that kid will eat anything on a dare. I told Greg to get rid of those stupid marbles years ago but he had to hang onto something from his childhood. Kids don't even play marbles anymore.…I don't know. Do you have anything from your childhood? Anything sentimental?

AKOSUA: I once found a rock shaped like a heart on the beach. I've been looking for another one ever since.

LEILA: Where is it?

AKOSUA: *(She shakes her head and goes back to cleaning.)* Some secrets should remain your own, Mrs. Tate, or else what do you have?

LEILA: *(Sighs.)* I need inspiration. I don't care where I find it at this point. What was your favourite food?

AKOSUA: *(Becoming quite animated.)* It's funny you ask because I woke up wanting my mommie's fufu, sweet potatoes and oxtail. I could taste it when I came out of my dream and it made me so sad that I could not have it.

LEILA: Fufu is…?

AKOSUA: It's something we make out of cassava and flour. You pick it up, roll it in a little ball and dip it in your stew and gravy. It's delicious.

LEILA: Fufu…

AKOSUA: It also means gay or homosexual to some people, but when I say it I'm talking about the food.

LEILA: Soon. You'll have it sooner than you think because you'll be home for Christmas. I know it's premature but that's your Christmas present. That's what Greg and I are giving you. A trip home!

AKOSUA: Oh, thank you so much! I know I haven't been here long, but I have to admit to being a little homesick.

LEILA: Of course that means we'll be putting off opening a bank account for you until the new year. A trip to Ghana is super expensive, especially at Christmas. You understand?

AKOSUA: Uh… I guess so. So, I won't get paid?

LEILA: Well, we could prorate your salary, since you started the last week of August, but then we'd have to subtract the cost of the flight here and that was…that was pricey! STEEP! Basically, you'd be left with nothing.

AKOSUA: Oh.

LEILA: Oh, honey! Canada, especially Toronto, is hella expensive. Tack on airfare, food, clothes…don't get me started. But if you want the money, then that's not a problem. You can still go home, but you'll have to pay for it. I'm sorry.

AKOSUA: Yes, of course.

LEILA: It's like a game show here! Do I take the trip or do I take the money? Right? Amiright??

AKOSUA: I will take the trip. Thank you so much. Oh yes, of course.

LEILA: You know, I think this little chat has inspired me. My juices are flowing. My creative juices, you know? Wow. Look at the time. I think it's time for you to unpack the dishwasher. But before you do I think you should take off that bracelet. The friendship bracelet Maggie gave you or, what did you call her?

AKOSUA: Magpie.

LEILA: Yeah, Magpie. I'd hate for it to slip off and get into the gears of the dishwasher or something. Here. I'll take it. *(She reaches out for it.)*

AKOSUA: *(Removes the bracelet reluctantly and hands it to LEILA.)* She gave it to me for good luck.

LEILA: Oh, how sweet. You're with your family and that's all the luck you'll need. *(She turns back to her laptop and begins typing.)* And can you bring me a water when you're done? Thanks, hun.

AKOSUA: Yes, yes…of course.

*AKOSUA exits. As she turns the corner, and out of AKOSUA's sight, LEILA slips the bracelet on her wrist and admires it before resuming typing.*

## Scene 8

*GREG and LEILA are in the kitchen. It's tense. AKOSUA is cleaning. She has become "furniture," in that they speak as though she is not there.*

GREG: I feel like you're yelling at me.

LEILA: I'm not, Greg. I'm just…frustrated. I'm – I can't… my novel is stalled, I couldn't find teacher gifts for Mrs. Elder and Mr. Frauts, and now you're telling me you're not going to be here at Christmas.

GREG: No, that's not what I said. I said that I will be here for Christmas, we'll open presents at your parents' place on Christmas Eve, like usual, have Christmas Day here so the kids can open their presents under the tree, I'll make a big pancake breakfast, you don't have to do anything, and then on Boxing Day I have to get ready to fly out for a conference. I have no choice in the matter.

LEILA: Yes, you do. You could say no.

GREG: Ley.

LEILA: Don't fucking call me that. I hate that nickname.

GREG: All right. Leila. I have to do this. This is my boss instructing me to go.

LEILA: Is she going?

GREG: Janice? No. It's Christmas.

*LEILA glares at him.*

What? What do you want? If she goes with me then I'm having an affair with her and if she's not I'm a pussy for going? What is it? Make up your fucking mind. Jesus!

LEILA: Me and the kids without you at Christmas? That's going to be so hard. They're home for like, three weeks, I can't do it alone.

GREG: Get Akosua to help you. That's why she's here, for God's sake.

LEILA: *(Lowering her voice.)* I told her she could have the holidays off.

GREG: She doesn't even celebrate Christmas. Hey, Akosua, sorry for bothering you. Would it be okay if we postponed your Christmas holidays until after December? I have a business trip that I have to go on and Leila will be overwhelmed with the kids.

LEILA: No, I won't be, Greg, I – don't make it sound like I can't take care of my own kids. Fuck.

GREG: Forgive my wife's language.

LEILA: Don't apologize for me, Greg. Don't do that. I am more than capable of policing my own language and... *(Pause.)* ...okay...I'm sorry.

AKOSUA: *(Stops what she's doing.)* It's fine. I don't mind.

GREG: See! Stress over nothing.

LEILA: I don't think there's anything wrong with wanting my husband home for Christmas, but that's okay, the maid is a fine substitute.

*LEILA storms out of the room. There is a very long pause as AKOSUA continues to clean.*

GREG: Sorry about that.

AKOSUA: It's none of my business.

*AKOSUA exits and walks to her room. It is time for her prayers. She pulls out her prayer rug, unaware that GREG has followed her.*

What are you doing?

GREG: *(Startled.)* Oh!

AKOSUA: What are you doing?

GREG: I'm sorry. I was just…I shouldn't be in here?

AKOSUA: It's your home, you can go wherever you want.

*There is a long pause.*

GREG: I'm sorry about…that. *(Gesturing off-stage.)*

AKOSUA: Mrs. Tate has given me the rest of the day off but if you'd like me to get you something –

GREG: No no no…ah no. Just, relax. I'm sorry. I'm kind of in the doghouse, as you can see… I came here just to see what you'd done with the room and it looks good, considering…the rug, I wasn't sure if we gave you that or –

AKOSUA: It's mine.

GREG: I see. *(He reaches out to touch it.)*

AKOSUA: *(She pulls back.)* I brought it with me from home.

GREG: I'm sorry.

AKOSUA: Why do you keep apologizing?

GREG: I'm Canadian. It's a bad habit. *(Laughs awkwardly.)* No. I mean, I shouldn't have come in here and touched your stuff. I used to hate it when my sister would go through my things.

AKOSUA: Touched my stuff?

GREG: Nothing.

AKOSUA: This is not "stuff." It is my prayer rug. I pray to Allah on this rug.

GREG: Ahh… Like Brody on *Homeland*.

AKOSUA: What?

GREG: Nothing. Just a TV show I'm watching.

AKOSUA: This is life, Mr. Tate, not television.

GREG: Yes, I'm sorry, I understand that, I was just trying to…relate, to *(Sighs.)*… I don't know….

AKOSUA: *(Softening a little, she pulls out the rug and shows it to GREG.)* Do you see this here? That must always be pointed to Mecca when I pray. Do you know where Mecca is?

*GREG shakes his head and AKOSUA regards him for a moment.*

Where are you from?

GREG: What do you mean?

AKOSUA: I mean, where are you from?

GREG: Nova Scotia. Eastern Canada.

AKOSUA: Your people, Mr. Tate, where are your people from?

GREG: Listen, I was born here. My mother was born here –

AKOSUA: She is white?

GREG: Yes/So?

AKOSUA: Oh/Okay.

GREG: Okay what?

AKOSUA: I do not mean any disrespect, Mr. Tate, but you do not appear to be a man who is very grounded. You are not really here.

GREG: –

AKOSUA: You are always looking at your phone, or playing games, or just not here. Unhappiness hangs around you like a shroud. The sun, the sky, your family are all right in front of you if you just look up. What more do you need?

GREG: I'm…no…no, that's not true. I'm preoccupied with work.

AKOSUA: Ah.. you use work as an excuse a lot, Mr. Tate. I work here all day and still find time to pray five times a day. Why have you strayed from your faith?

GREG: There weren't a lot of black Jews in Nova Scotia. Christians, yes, Catholics, Baptists, absolutely, but Jewish? Not really. My mother tried but it just… *(He shakes his head.)* I didn't even get a bar mitzvah. I moved to Toronto as soon as I turned eighteen and never looked back.

AKOSUA: There are black Jews all over Africa. You should go for a visit and find a way to reconnect with your heritage. You escape your home and your religion but you cannot run from yourself. You need to find Mecca within yourself, Mr. Tate, because once you do you will no longer lie to your wife.

GREG: Who says I lie to my wife?

AKOSUA: Mr. Tate, you are not going on a business trip.

GREG: What? You don't know what you're talking about.

AKOSUA: No. You are right. I do not know. I must have misunderstood what I heard when you were on the phone with your friend. Your wife mentioned you could be indecisive sometimes.

GREG: I'm sorry?

AKOSUA: South Beach, yes?

*They eye one another steadily.*

GREG: You're not married. Sometimes spouses need a break. I mean, my wife loves me, but there are some things that she doesn't have to know. For the good of the marriage, you understand?

AKOSUA: Mhmm.

GREG: What does that mean?

AKOSUA: Nothing.

GREG: I'm not gay.

AKOSUA: Okay.

GREG: You don't believe me.

AKOSUA: It doesn't matter what I believe.

GREG: I can prove it.

AKOSUA: It doesn't matter to me.

GREG: I can show you. I can prove I'm not gay.

AKOSUA: What does that mean?

*GREG takes a step towards AKOSUA and she backs up.*

Mr. Tate!

GREG: *(Shrinking back.)* I wasn't going to hurt you. I just wanted to – Please don't tell my wife.

AKOSUA: If you keep lying you will begin to feel trapped. Holding onto a lie is like a cancer, Mr. Tate; it will eat you from the inside out.

GREG: Sometimes I think about the things I haven't told her and they just sit right here in the middle of my chest like a lodestone. It's heavy and hot and I need to use all kinds of things to distract me from it. Do you know what I mean?

AKOSUA: I just know that it is hard to keep lies straight; they get all tangled.

GREG: Well, thank you, and sorry about cancelling the trip; couldn't be helped. I'll make sure Leila adds a bonus to your next paycheque to make up for the disappointment. Oh, and speaking of tangles, I got rid of that nasty spider and its web in the corner there. The web was ginormous. I figured you didn't get rid of it because it was too high.

AKOSUA: I –

GREG: No need to thank me. Enjoy the rest of your day off.

AKOSUA: Thank you, Mr. Tate.

GREG: Call me Greg.

*GREG exits. AKOSUA smiles until he is out of sight. She looks to the upper right corner of the room where the spider was and then looks at the audience.*

## Scene 9

*Same day. GREG enters the bedroom where LEILA is typing furiously into her laptop. There's a scented candle burning on the bedside table. He sits down on the bed and waits for her to look up. He's holding a ZenSoy pudding for her and looks at her with puppy dog eyes.*

GREG: I know you never eat these, but what's a little cheat once in a while, right?

LEILA: You can't bribe me.

GREG: I know.

LEILA: I'm really angry at you, Greg.

GREG: I know. Could you look at me, please?

LEILA: Can't. I'm on a roll here. It's amazing how creative I can be when I'm angry.

GREG: Then you should have a collection of novels by now, huh? *(Chuckles.)*

LEILA: *(Stops, turns, and glares at him.)* Do you really think now is the time to make jokes at my expense. Really?

GREG: *(Dropping his head in his hands.)* Leila. I… Why does this have to be so hard?

LEILA: You're making this hard and, you know what, I'm not sure how this is hard on you. You! I'm the stay-at-home mom and I'm the one writing a book.

GREG: And maybe you should stop.

LEILA: What?

GREG: You're not happy. Just because you believe you should write a book doesn't mean you drop everything to do it when it's clearly making you miserable. What did Christopher Hitchens say, "Everyone has a book in them and, in most cases, that's where it should stay"?

LEILA: You want me to go back to work.

GREG: I want you to be happy or at least not so frustrated all the time. Tell me you don't miss it.

LEILA: I do miss going to a job where I know what I'm doing, but I made a commitment to finish this and I'm going to follow through.

GREG: All right.

LEILA: I need your support.

GREG: You have it. You always have.

LEILA: Maybe I should take a creative writing class... Maybe I need to get out of the house for a little bit every day and write in a different environment...

GREG: And now that Akosua is completely trained, you can let her go pick up the kids from school, perhaps start dinner while you're out.

LEILA: Oh...about Akosua –

GREG: She and I just had a talk, things got a little tense –

LEILA: Oh no!

GREG: And I need to talk to you about something.

LEILA: Oh....

GREG: Please, sit.

*LEILA moves to sit on the bed beside GREG.*

You've probably noticed that I've been a little preoccupied and distant.

LEILA: Mmmhmm...but that's because of work, right?

GREG: No. That's been an excuse.

LEILA: Oh...

GREG: Leila...

LEILA: Oh nooo…

GREG: I miss Judaism.

LEILA: What?

GREG: I've been thinking about it since Akosua showed up and you said I wasn't really a Jew.

LEILA: Well, you…it's not like you've ever been very Jewish.

GREG: See, I don't like it when you say things like that because it's dismissive.

LEILA: You've never talked about this before. Where's this coming from? You want to be Jewish now?

GREG: Now? I AM Jewish.

LEILA: Okay, okay, you're Jewish, so, now what? You want to go to synagogue? You want to give Christopher a bar mitzvah? *(Snorts.)*

GREG: *(Unsmiling.)* He is going to be thirteen in a few years.

LEILA: *(Horrified.)* No! I mean…Greg! I'm not Jewish and I'm not converting. *(Pause.)* Do you want me to convert?

GREG: You don't have to convert, unless you want to.

*LEILA says nothing.*

Leila, I don't know how this could work but I think that it can.

LEILA: *(Despairing.)* I just don't understand where this is coming from and – *(Gasps.)* Do you want to cancel Christmas?

GREG: Leila, no. But –

LEILA: No tree?

GREG: *(Takes her by both hands.)* NO! Please. Breathe. *(Pause.)* When I was a kid, Shabbat was a comforting ritual. My mom would make sure we were there to watch her light the candle every Friday night, and even though I was ambivalent about being Jewish I loved that one constant in my life. I'm not asking to cancel Christmas, stop eating bacon, or any other crazy idea you think I have. But I do want our kids to have some idea of their Jewish history, and lighting the Shabbat candles followed by a nice dinner with wine....a little challah...it would be a start. Usually it's the woman of the house who lights the candles but I can do it, I think. I'll call my mom and ask.

LEILA: You want to call your mom?

GREG: You always tell me I should do it more often and now I have a reason to reconnect.

LEILA: I'm going to need some time to think about this.

GREG: This is something small, Leila. We get together on Fridays, as a family, and right before sunset we light the candles. That's it.

LEILA: That's it.

GREG: I'll never stay late at the office on Fridays again and it'll be a good way for you and Maggie to bond. The mother always teaches the daughter about this.

LEILA: Hmm.

GREG: And, hey, this could be good material for your book. Or your second book, once you finish this one.

LEILA: *(Brightening.)* You believe I can finish my book?

GREG: Of course I do.

LEILA: *(Thinking for a bit.)* Okay. Okay. I'll go shopping for some candles. We can do the lighting thing...soon.

GREG: *(Smiling.)* And to think this all happened because of Akosua.

*GREG gets up and starts changing.*

LEILA: *(Starts.)* I'm sorry, what does she have to do with it?

GREG: It sounds crazy, but her being so religious made me wonder if maybe I was missing something in my life. Imagine that…a Muslim inspiring me to be more Jewish. *(Smiles and shakes his head.)*

LEILA: Imagine that.

GREG: You were so right in hiring her.

LEILA: Huh.

*GREG kisses LEILA on the cheek.*

GREG: I'm going to take a shower. And Leila, thank you, I love you.

*GREG exits.*

LEILA: Love you, too.

*LEILA blows out the candle on the bedside table.*

## Scene 10

*It's now the new year. AKOSUA is in the study cleaning. There's a menorah on top of the shelf and a laptop open on the desk. It is LEILA's novel. AKOSUA tries not to look at it but she can't help it, sits down and begins to read.*

LEILA: Sorry to bother you again. I'm – I'm…what are you doing?

AKOSUA: I was just –

LEILA: You read some of my book?

AKOSUA: The laptop was open and I –

LEILA: What did you think?

AKOSUA: I am sorry, Mrs. Tate, but what you have written is so wrong.

LEILA: Wrong? What do you know about writing?

AKOSUA: Nothing, but I am a Ghanaian and that story you've written trivializes history.

LEILA: What?

AKOSUA: A slave is brought to a castle and treated like a princess by a slave trader on the Ivory Coast? That is awful.

LEILA: Oh, don't start with that "I'm pissed because my great-great-great-great-great grandmother was a slave," argument because I don't feel sympathetic to that at all. I studied African history. I've done charity work in Africa and I know the history of slavery.

AKOSUA: Really? What do you know? Tell me.

*LEILA pauses and is at a momentary loss for words.*

LEILA: I'm writing historical fiction, Akosua. If I want Christopher Columbus to sweep in and save the day I can do that, because it's fiction set in a real historical period.

AKOSUA: Those castles in Accra had dungeons filled with slaves. Overcrowded, stinking, covered in piss, shit, and frightened at what was going to happen to them. And terrible things did happen to those people, Mrs. Tate. They were not characters in a fairy tale. Nobody saved them and nobody was turned into a princess.

LEILA: I didn't say that and I seem to have struck a nerve and… Why am I arguing with my maid?!

AKOSUA: Because we are family, right? I should be able to be open with you, right?

LEILA: *(Apprehensively.)* Right…

AKOSUA: So, let me be blunt and ask you if you have any plans to pay me.

LEILA: I'm sorry?

AKOSUA: I have been here working for you and your family for almost six months and I have not been paid.

LEILA: What?!

AKOSUA: Every time I ask about getting paid you come up with some excuse.

LEILA: *(She sits down in the chair.)* Yes, of course… I'm sorry we couldn't send you home at Christmas, but you understand, right? Money is tight. With the kids' swimming lessons, hockey, soccer… and now Christopher needs braces…it goes on and on.

AKOSUA: When are you going to pay me?

LEILA: Pay you?

AKOSUA: I work for you, you pay me, that is what I expect.

LEILA: You call living in Canada with a roof over your head and full-time work nothing? Back in Africa you didn't have anything close to this.

AKOSUA: You don't know what I had in Ghana. I would have been paid and I would be free to come and go as I please.

LEILA: Your payment is room and board. Your payment is – is – is…uh, getting some very important skills in how to run a household. Do you have any idea how expensive it was to bring you here? Your work visa, the plane ticket, the paperwork, clothes for winter? Boots? And…well…feeding you! That all costs us, you know. It's like we have three kids instead of two.

AKOSUA: You call me family but do not let me use the same dishes. You will not let me leave the house unless you are with me.

LEILA: This is my house and I can do what I like. I don't want you using the same dishes as us, no. I keep you inside for your own safety.

AKOSUA: Mrs. Tate –

LEILA: *(Snaps.)* How many times do I have to tell you to call me Leila! *(While speaking she stands up, looks in the "mirror" which is the audience and pulls a hair elastic off her wrist. Begins to put her hair in a ponytail.)* Please. *(She takes some lipstick out of her purse and applies it.)* Has Greg…has he come to see you? I mean, outside of when he should see you, does he – Okay. Um…this is not… He's been cheating again. Not on me. I mean, in a way, he has but I'm talking about smoking. He's been smoking again. I can taste it when he kisses me. Black licorice. Black licorice and nicotine. He eats the candy because he thinks it will cover up the tar, but I know. I know he's cheating again because that's the only time he eats candy. I've heard that alcoholics drink vodka because it doesn't have a scent, but it does. It absolutely stinks and that kind of deception is almost worse. *(Pause.)* I am trying to protect you.

AKOSUA: You do not want me to escape.

LEILA: *(Laughs derisively.)* Escape?!

AKOSUA: You do not trust me, I am not allowed outside and you have not paid me since I came here to work for you. Work without pay is –

LEILA: Is what?

AKOSUA: It is wrong.

LEILA: Okay, let me see here. I talked to a friend about this the other day, a black friend, I might add, and I think you'll find this interesting. She told me that her aunt, who lives in Nigeria, by the way, picked up a homeless girl on the street, brought her home, gave her a bed and food and instructed her in how to clean house. That girl is grateful. She does not think of herself as a slave.

AKOSUA: Your friend and her aunt can call it whatever they want, but it is still slavery under a different name. Give me my passport.

LEILA: I gave it to Greg. He knows where it is. Besides, I don't know where you think you can go. You can't survive here without money or connections.

AKOSUA: I thought you said I was your family and that we are here to take care of each other. What happened to that?

LEILA: I am trying to take care of you, Akosua. I am. We're going to pay you.

AKOSUA: You really do believe that I am a stupid country girl.

LEILA: Not stupid. A little naïve, maybe. My friend's aunt has it all figured out. That girl can come and go as she pleases. She's never beaten or locked up. She never has to worry about sexual advances. She's safe.

AKOSUA: So, I should be happy that you do not beat me? That I am not chained to the wall or threatened with rape? Those things make what you are doing okay?

LEILA: Don't twist my words.

AKOSUA: Please let me go. I will walk out of here with nothing, Leila. I do not need you to free me.

LEILA: Okay, but just remember that most people in Canada don't even know girls like you exist. You don't exist. Not here, anyway. If you tell anyone anything about being kept here, you're the one who's going to be punished, not me. You don't want to be sent back to Ghana, do you? I'm just looking out for you.

AKOSUA: You are looking out for me? *(She is standing beside LEILA's laptop now.)*

LEILA: Of course.

AKOSUA: Well, let me show you the same respect. *(She sits down at the laptop and begins typing.)* Your husband said you were strong-minded so…

LEILA: What do you mean? What are you doing? How do you know my password?

AKOSUA: I don't. I know Mr. Tate's. You did not really think that because I am from a Third World country I do not know how to use a computer, did you?

*AKOSUA is searching for a site.*

LEILA: Akosua…

*AKOSUA turns the laptop towards LEILA, showing her a website.*

AKOSUA: Your husband is not who you think he is.

*LEILA sits down, begins scrolling through and looks up at AKOSUA. She gets up, pulls AKOSUA's passport from underneath the menorah, and hands it to her. She goes back to the computer, turns her back on AKOSUA and continues scrolling through.*

GREG: (*O/S.*) Leila! Are you home? There was a fire drill at work so Janice let us go early, and as I was driving home the rest of that Gwendolyn MacEwen poem popped into my head. Hey, Akosua!

*GREG enters as AKOSUA exits.*

"You held out the light, you held out the light to light my cigarette…" Anyways, the end is "Now it's always the same no matter where we meet, you burn me" Ouch!

*GREG kisses LEILA and pulls her hair out of the ponytail.*

Whatcha lookin' at?

*GREG sees the screen; he and LEILA look at each other.*

I can explain.

*What follows is a stylized, slow-motion pantomime of the beginning of a violent fight.*

## Scene 11

*Dark stage.*

DISPATCHER: 911, what is your emergency?

WITNESS: I think something bad has happened at my neighbours' house.

DISPATCHER: Yes.

WITNESS: There were bodies…I think they're dead. I think my neighbours are dead.

DISPATCHER: Please don't go into the house, ma'am. The police are on their way. What is your name, ma'am?

WITNESS: Nansi.

DISPATCHER: Can I get a last name?

*Dial tone.*

## Scene 12

*A dark stage except for AKOSUA in a pool of light. There is a piece of luggage at her feet.*

AKOSUA: Do you know the story of the spider god Anansi? Anansi is very famous in Africa. Long, long ago Anansi was walking in the bush. Soon she came upon a house with a very, very, VERY old man sitting on the porch. "Good day, sir! I have been walking all morning and would love to have a cool drink of water." The old man said nothing. Anansi, who thought that the old man might have been deaf, repeated in a loud voice, "GOOD MORNING, SIR! MAY I HAVE A DRINK OF WATER?" Still, nothing. Anansi shrugged, went into the house and not only helped herself to water but as much food as she could eat. When she finished eating she went outside to see the old man sitting in the same spot. Anansi thanked him for his hospitality and returned home. Anansi returned to this man's home several times and even brought her daughter to him as a gift. The old man still said nothing. How rude! The next day when Anansi went back to the old man's house she could not find her daughter. Where was she? She looked everywhere but was unable to find her.

Anansi rushed outside, grabbed the old man by the collar and yelled, "Where is my daughter?" Finally, the old man spoke in a deep raspy voice. "Do... you... know... who... I... am?" "Yes," Anansi said. "You are a kind old man."

"Hah!!" the old man rasped. "My name is Death and *you* came looking for me." She ran as fast as she could, but wherever Anansi turned, Death was right behind. Finally, she bolted for her home and climbed up into the ceiling. Death exhaled, looked up at the ceiling and smiled, showing all thirty-seven-and-a-half teeth. And, as he set a giant barrel of flour under Anansi, she dropped on top of Death's head, dunking his face into the flour, and ran for her life.

Death has never caught Anansi the Spider. So, whenever you see spider webs on the ceiling, they belong to her, and she is still trying to get away from Death. And never forget: When you dig a hole for someone, you are sure to fall into it yourself.

*Percussive music rises as the spotlight shrinks.*

*The end.*

# EATING POMEGRANATES NAKED

"If you are silent about your pain,
they'll kill you and say you enjoyed it."

– Zora Neale Hurston

# Production History

*Eating Pomegranates Naked* debuted at the SummerWorks Performance Festival in Toronto, Ontario in August of 2013 with the following team:

RUSHTON Bailey............. Awaovieyi Agie

SCOTT Hansa.................................Eli Ham

SERA Hansa...................... Marci T. House

CASSIDY Lam...................... Susan A. Lock

ANAAR Bailey.............Cherissa Richards

Directed by: Mumbi Tindyebwa Otu

Set and Costume: Joanna Yu

Sound Design: Thomas Ryder Payne

Lighting Design: Siobhán Sleath

Stage Manager: Lois Dawson

Anaar (Cherissa Richards), Rushton (Awaovieyi Agie), Cassidy (Susan A. Lock), Sera (Marci T. House), and Scott (Eli Ham), enjoying a lovely dinner before all hell breaks loose.
*Photo by Lauren Vandenbrook.*

Someone has a secret and Anaar (Cherissa Richards) may not be able to keep it to herself.
*Photo by Lauren Vandenbrook.*

# Characters

SERA Hansa:
Black woman, late 30s.
Teacher, fiery temper. She is a swan.

SCOTT Hansa:
SERA's husband, white, late 30s.
Marketing executive.

ANAAR Bailey:
RUSHTON's wife, biracial, late 20s.
Bubbly, young energy, former model.
She is a flamboyant peacock.

Dr. RUSHTON Bailey:
ANAAR's husband, dark-skinned black, late 30s.
An immunologist.

CASSIDY Lam:
SERA's best friend, Hakka-Chinese-Jamaican,
late 30s woman, loud, gregarious.
A chunk of indigo-coloured hair. Artist.
Can break into Jamaican patois when angered.
The personality of a grackle.

# Act One

## Scene 1

*The stage is black.*

ANAAR: Stop it.

RUSHTON: What?

ANAAR: Stop it!

RUSHTON: Really?

ANAAR: I'm tired…let me…quit it!

*Lights up stage left. ANAAR, a beautiful biracial woman is in bed with her husband, RUSHTON, a dark-skinned black man.*

RUSHTON: I can't imagine a better way to wake up…

ANAAR: Maybe for you, but not at five in the morning. On a Wednesday.

RUSHTON: I have to go to work. I'm up, you're up, and you never usually complain…

ANAAR: Babe, I'm not up and that's not how Hump Day got its name. Please don't turn this into something I want.

RUSHTON: Aw, come on, don't act like you haven't enjoyed morning sex before. I know you love it…

ANAAR: Okay, sweetie, this isn't about me not loving it. I love it on Saturday morning, Sunday morning, on my day off even but, shit, we went to bed just six hours ago. I'm exhausted. Besides, it's not morning to me if the sun hasn't come up. Drop it.

RUSHTON: *(Sighs.)* All right.

ANAAR: When you get home from work I'll make it up to you. Promise.

RUSHTON: Are we having less sex now?

ANAAR: What?

RUSHTON: I swear we had more sex when we first got married. Am I imagining this? Is it me? You don't think I'm attractive anymore.

ANAAR: You're the handsomest man in the world and I can't keep my hands off of you but just not now. Please let me sleep! I'm not awake enough to have this conversation.

RUSHTON: Okay, okay… I'm going to take a shower.

*ANAAR has already rolled over and fallen asleep. RUSHTON looks at her for a long time, adjusts himself, turns off the side lamp on the nightstand and walks offstage to the bathroom for his shower. The sound of a shower starts up. The alarm comes on and ANAAR slams it off and covers her head with the sheets. RUSHTON comes back onstage in a towel. He gets dressed during the following conversation.*

Babe. Babe. Anaar?

ANAAR: *(From under the covers.)* Hm?

RUSHTON: Sorry. I know you're trying to sleep but I just noticed you're out of tampons. Do you want me to pick up a box on the way home from work for you?

ANAAR: Uh…sure. Ya, ya, thanks.

RUSHTON: What kind do you like again?

ANAAR: I don't care. Whatever.

RUSHTON: With applicator? No applicator?

ANAAR: Mm.

RUSHTON: We're trying to be good to the environment so no applicator. And I'll pick up the organic cotton ones you like. Is that okay?

ANAAR: Mmhmm.

RUSHTON: All right, my beautiful tulip, I'll leave you to sleep.

*RUSHTON pulls the sheet off ANAAR, kisses her shoulder.*

See you tonight.

ANAAR: Mm.

*RUSHTON exits. We hear the front door slam shut. ANAAR sits up. She's wide awake.*

Fuck!

## Scene 2

*Same day. This is the workout room in SCOTT's house. "All Eyez on Me" by Tupac is playing while SCOTT works out. He's seriously strength-training and periodically takes breaks to rap along with Pac. His wife SERA walks in unnoticed. She stands and watches him for a few seconds, walks over to the stereo, and shuts it off.*

SERA: Looking good, sir. Sorry to bug you, but I just wanted to know if there's anything you wanted in particular for the dinner on Friday night.

SCOTT: Friday?

SERA: Yeah, two days from now. The dinner party we're having for our friends, remember?

SCOTT: Shit! Right, right.

SERA: You did invite Rush and his wife, right?

SCOTT: Yup, they're coming.

SERA: There's just something about her that rubs me the wrong way.

SCOTT: It's because she used to be a model and you think she's a moron. You're a hater.

SERA: Nah nah, just because I don't like a good-looking woman – and she's not that pretty, by the way – just because I don't like her doesn't mean – You don't have to automatically go to the obvious "pretty girl hate" theory. Please.

*The next two speeches are delivered simultaneously.*

SCOTT:
No? It's not because she's a light-skinned model, ten years younger than you, married to our doctor friend?

SERA:
Former model! Give me some credit, Scott! And he's an immunologist, not a real doctor.

SCOTT: Just cut her some slack on Friday. Rush has never been this happy. Please, babe? I'm going to ask you to practise that Christian charity I know dwells in that dark heart of yours. Sheathe your sword. We don't see her all that often anyway.

SERA: I never called her a moron.

SCOTT: *(Laughs.)* Yes, you did. Whenever she posts something on Facebook and the words are spelled wrong –

SERA: It said, "What am I going to wear tonight?" and wear was spelled "w-e-r-e."

SCOTT: So she's not as smart as you, let it go.

SERA: I called her "dumb-dumb." Not a moron. Dumb-dumb is way nicer.

SCOTT: I'll remember to call her that as I take her coat. Is Cassidy coming?

SERA: She said she'd be here. No date.

SCOTT: As per usual.

SERA: What does that mean?

SCOTT: I love Cassidy. I think she's one of the best friends you have, but she's harsh sometimes, like, she has no censor. Loud, abrasive and, I think, well, I think she's a bit of a thief.

SERA: Not this again.

SCOTT: I can't believe you refuse to side with me on this one.

SERA: Cass and I have been friends for over ten years and I know her. I know her so well that I'd swear on my life that she didn't take your butter.

SCOTT: Organic, fifteen-dollars-a-pound Irish butter. It wasn't just butter. It was ambrosia.

SERA: Okay, first of all, sometimes you are such a girl. Second of all, you work out like a friggin' maniac, drink protein shakes, cut out pork, and stopped smoking, so how does butter get a pass? Thirdly, who the fuck steals butter?

SCOTT: Woman, I am the manliest motherfucker you are ever going to meet. Let's just clear that up right now. If I'm gonna have a guilty pleasure I think a schmear of fresh, creamy butter on a slab of hot sourdough once in a while is all right. It's something I do for myself that nobody else can understand. Except Cassidy, of course, because she stole my fuckin' butter.

SERA: I'll ask her.

SCOTT: Don't. Her high cholesterol will be her punishment.

SERA: No. This is a mystery that I have to solve. She's the only person who has a key to our place, so it's possible but not likely.

SCOTT: Just don't. I don't want things to get weird. I'm over it. See? Now if you don't mind, I should get back to creating the body beautiful for you.

SERA: Yeah, right. For me. Dinner on Friday. What do you think? Chicken, pasta, or steak?

SCOTT: Definitely no pasta. Could you make your world-famous jerk chicken? You haven't made that in ages. Some rice and peas, maybe fried plantain. What do you think?

SERA: I think it will be very easy for Anaar to puke it all up after dinner.

SCOTT: You're so mean!

SERA: That's why you love me. Fruit or cake for dessert?

SCOTT: Lemon chiffon, please.

SERA: If they have it. *(She kisses him and walks over to the stereo.)* Love you. *(Turns the music back on.)* Don't forget to stretch.

*SCOTT goes back to his workout. The music is loud. SERA watches SCOTT for a minute before turning to leave.*

## Scene 3

*Same day, later in the morning.*

*SERA is standing and pacing in the schoolyard watching the kids play at recess. Her arms are crossed and she looks grim. The sound of kids laughing and running around the tarmac plays softly underneath.*

SERA: No no no no no! Madison, get down from there! Get down. Don't make me come over there. Your mom told me not to let you on the jungle gym after you broke your arm last year. So down, now! Thank you. *(Walks a little bit and then spots a child doing something she doesn't like.)* Harlan, Harlan. Yes, I'm talking to you. What are you doing? Yeah, I see that you're doing nothing. Why? See, this is recess, so you should be up, running around, playing with other kids. I dunno, just get up off of the ground and get some exercise. The fresh air isn't enough. Don't be silly, everyone has friends. Look at all those kids. Talk to them. Do it. Get up! I'm watching you. Yeah, that's it. Go ask Madison about her broken arm. She loves talking about herself. Mm hmm. There ya go.

*CASSIDY, SERA's best friend, has walked onto the schoolyard behind SERA, unbeknownst to her. She's wearing camouflage cargo pants, a plain white tee, pink Keds, and giant colourful jewellery.*

*(Mumbling to herself.)* Filthy cockroaches and lazy turtles, all of them. My lord.

CASSIDY: Whoa! Don't hold back, Sister!

SERA: *(Startled.)* How long have you been standing there?

CASSIDY: Having a bad day?

SERA: You! Mister, drop the rock. Go inside. Recess is over for you. Move! Don't make me come over there, boy! That's right. March. Lawd have mercy, these kids are trying to kill me or get me fired.

CASSIDY: You're having a shitty day. I get it. It's a good thing you have a friend like me. Look what I brought ya.

*CASSIDY hands SERA a paper bag.*

SERA: Are these my favourite oatmeal cookies? It's not a G&T, but it'll do.

CASSIDY: It's 10:30 in the morning!

SERA: It's five o'clock somewhere. I don't know how their parents stand them sometimes.

CASSIDY: They don't. They enroll them in Spanish classes, sign language classes, how to be the next overpaid CEO classes. Can you believe there are tweens learning how to appreciate *foie gras* and shuck oysters? When I was in school my parents didn't care where I was as long I wasn't doing drugs; now kids are scheduled within a minute of their lives.

SERA: It's no wonder they run around like crazy little hooligans. Freedom! I just don't want to be their indulgent but stern mommy, you know? Anyway, dinner this Friday. I'm looking forward to this first dinner party in our new house.

CASSIDY: Should be fun. It's just me, Rushton, and his wife, right?

SERA: Yup.

CASSIDY: The try-hard.

SERA: Right.

CASSIDY: I can't wait to meet her.

SERA: *(Eating a cookie.)* These are amazing.

CASSIDY: I use real vanilla. And butter.

SERA: Yeah?

CASSIDY: Nothing but the best for my princess.

SERA: Why do I feel like you want something?

CASSIDY: Because you're paranoid.

SERA: What are you doing here, anyway?

CASSIDY: Substitute teaching. Art class.

SERA: They couldn't just cancel the class and give the kids a spare?

CASSIDY: Our education dollars at work, everybody. *(She does a slow clap to an imaginary audience.)*

SERA: I'm just saying what everybody is thinking.

CASSIDY: No, you're just being mean.

SERA: Scott said I was being mean, too.

CASSIDY: Your chi is off. It's been off for a while.

SERA: Since when did you become a sentient fortune cookie?

CASSIDY: Stop being racist. See, you are kinda mean.

SERA: I'm not in the mood for this conversation. Can you bring wine for the dinner?

CASSIDY: Red or white?

SERA: Anything, as long as it's not in a box.

CASSIDY: Snob.

SERA: I'm not drinking, so bring what you like.

CASSIDY: Oooh! Not drinking, huh?

SERA: Cassidy.

CASSIDY: Uh huh.

*The recess bell rings.*

SERA: Opa! That's my cue.

CASSIDY: Lunch later?

SERA: Sorry, can't. I have an errand I have to run. I'll see you at my place on Friday. Don't forget the wine!

*SERA exits while yelling at the kids.*

Let's go! Conor, Phillip, Ashley! Move it! I'm not asking you twice.

## Scene 4

*The nondescript interior of a boardroom. This is where SCOTT Hansa is presenting to a group of clients. The audience will function as the clients. There is a screen set up, upon which a series of images will be projected from a PowerPoint presentation. The images and SCOTT's voice are the primary focus of this scene; think TedTalks presentation.*

SCOTT: When I think of the saying "truth in advertising," all I can do is laugh. Laugh because advertising is predicated on a lie. A lie we all know is being perpetrated on the consumer. But let's not feel sorry for the consumer, because that unsuspecting individual standing in front of a urinal being bombarded with ads for cars, or the rider sitting in the subway looking at the banner promoting another feature on another expensive phone wants, no, *embraces* the assurances that are being presented in vibrant blue, red, and green.

You have an established base of customers who want and buy your product. No amount of advertising is going to change that fact. But you want that number to grow. Well, marketing and its sidekick, advertising, exist to widen the pool of potential consumers. How do we do this? McCann Erickson says that advertising is *Truth Told Well*. Basically, truth with spin. We tell a story. Because at the end of the day, people don't want to hear the real story. They want embellishment. Truth is harsh, and, let's be honest, it may force them to make a change or changes that they are not willing or can't afford to make.

For example.

*A slide of a picture of Breyers ice cream comes up on the screen.*

Let's look at this family treat that would please all but the lactose-intolerant. (*Folksy.*) Looks good, don't it? But if you look closer, right there in the bottom right-hand corner you will see in tiny letters, "frozen dessert." Now, what does that mean? Well, it looks like an ice cream container, and the picture on the box looks like ice cream and if I gave each of you a sample you may not even realize that what you are eating is not, in fact, ice cream. With corporations trying to save money and increase profits, ice cream just got too expensive to produce. So, companies like Breyers and Neilsen started placing these products in freezers all across the country. Suddenly you could get Neapolitan, Rocky Road, Vanilla, and Double Fudge Treats for just $2.99 a carton. What a deal!

> *We see the image of a person jumping in the air in excitement on a PowerPoint slide.*

Except, you weren't getting the real deal. Hydrogenated vegetable oil, fluffed up with air. That's what you get when you eat "frozen dessert," since FDA dictated that it couldn't be called ice cream when there was no cream present. That's why you can find a lot of frozen dessert in stores for $2.99 beside $8.99 real cream ice cream. But you know what? Breyers does very well in sales despite their fake treat while Chapmans, a company that only makes real ice cream, but rarely advertises, lags in their profits. But let's be honest, if you stopped a mother of three in the store reaching for a container of frozen dessert and explained the differences between that and the good stuff, do you think she'd shell out the extra five or six bucks? No – and that is an example of being faced with the truth and not being willing or able to change. You're all going to go home and look in your freezers now, aren't you?

My point is that we are surrounded by a world wherein people, consumers, will believe what they want, even if the truth is staring them in the face in an eighteen-point font. Lies are easier to stomach than the truth, which might explain why a lot of you are leaving before the end. *(SCOTT is getting uncomfortable, as he appears to be losing his audience.)* As a marketing and advertising firm we are always keeping an eye out for the best, the smartest and the least invasive manner to reach your customers. So, uh…print ads are just not good enough anymore. It's all about viral marketing now.

*We hear the sound of a door closing as people continue to leave the conference room.*

Now, there's a term that has been divorced of its true meaning.

*We see a PowerPoint image of the dictionary definition.*

…Wait a minute, have I done this part already?

*There is a long pause as he checks his notes and more people exit.*

Sorry, uh, viral is derived from virus, which is Latin for a slimy liquid, a poison; anything that corrupts or poisons the mind or character. Wow! *(Quietly to himself.)* That sounds terrible, why did I put that in? ….Wait, gentlemen, ladies, don't leave. I'm trying to – words change their meanings over time, that's what I'm trying to – and it's only in marketing, or art, for that matter, where something originally perceived as heinous can now be seen as desirable. Come on, don't, don't do this –

*We hear the sound of the final person leaving, and lights come up on SCOTT.*

Shit.

## Scene 5

*The sound of children on a playground starts softly and grows in volume until it's almost unbearable.*

*The stage is dark and a spotlight grows on a woman, SERA, centre stage, in the middle of a chant that turns to a primal scream.*

SERA: Holy Holy Holy is the Lord God Almighty. Holy Holy Holy is the Lord God Almighty. Holy Holy Holy…

*The sound and light effects should grow at exactly the same time to an unbearable pitch and cut out suddenly.*

## Scene 6

*We are in the dining room and the table is set for six. The dinner has been set on the table and everyone is seated. SERA is in white, ANAAR is wearing something tight and colourful. Everyone else is dressed casually. SERA and SCOTT are seated at either ends of the table, ANAAR and RUSHTON are sitting next to each other.*

SERA: All right, everyone, I'm just going to have to assume she's coming late. It's not like Cassidy not to call but I'm sure she'll have a good excuse.

RUSHTON: The food looks amazing so…

SCOTT: Go ahead. Babe, do you want me to put on some music? Babe?

*SERA has her head bowed.*

Sorry.

ANAAR: What?

SERA: Nothing. Just saying grace.

*CASSIDY enters wearing a bike helmet. She's cranky and a little bedraggled.*

CASSIDY: Well, thank god I'm here to elevate the intellectual discourse.

RUSHTON: How did you get in?

CASSIDY: I have a key.

SERA: You made it! What happened to you?

CASSIDY: I got doored on my way here.

ANAAR: Oh my God!

CASSIDY: I need a drink.

SCOTT: Red or white?

CASSIDY: I don't care.

*SCOTT pours her a glass of wine.*

Where's my seat? Why am I sitting by myself on this side of the table? Why are you two sitting side by side instead of across from one another like Scott and Sera?

SERA: Cass, relax. Are you okay? Should we take you to the hospital?

CASSIDY: No, no. I wasn't going that fast, and thankfully, I was wearing my helmet.

ANAAR: (*Rising and holding her hand out to shake hands.*) Hi, I'm Anaar. Rushton's wife.

CASSIDY: Hi, Anna.

ANAAR: Anaar.

RUSHTON: You'd know that if you had come to the wedding.

CASSIDY: I don't think I was invited. *(Looking at ANAAR.)* Do you remember my name on the guest list? Wow, you are really pretty.

ANAAR: Thank you. If you were doored, how did you get here?

SERA: You could have called and had one of us pick you up.

CASSIDY: I lost my phone. Maybe I left it at the bank machine, art supply store, or the liquor store, I dunno, because I can't call them. Did you know it costs fifty cents to make a call from a pay phone, IF you can find one?

SCOTT: Do pay phones even exist anymore? Did you find one?

CASSIDY: No, not immediately, because the assumption is that everyone has a cellphone. Eventually I did find one but once I found enough change – and FYI, those machines won't take dimes or nickels – I realized that I didn't know your number.

SERA: You couldn't remember our number?

CASSIDY: No. I don't actually KNOW it. Our dependence on smartphones has made us idiots without the ability to retain basic information. I barely remember my number. What's my phone number?

SERA: I have no flippin' idea.

CASSIDY: And we've known each other how long?

SERA: Since high school, and you always knew my number.

CASSIDY: 416-748-1338.

SERA: Wow!

CASSIDY: But iPhones didn't exist in the era of harem pants, banana clips, and typewriters.

ANAAR: You just have to use your memory like a muscle. That's what I do.

CASSIDY: My muscles are a little flabby these days, and we can't all be twenty-two.

ANAAR: I'm twenty-eight.

RUSHTON: And she used to be a model and an actress.

CASSIDY: So?

ANAAR: I *am* an actress, I mean actor.

CASSIDY: Which is it? Actor or actress?

ANAAR: My acting teacher used to say that an actress is a prostitute so…

CASSIDY: You're a prostitute?

RUSHTON: What did you say?

CASSIDY: Ooops! Sorry.

RUSHTON: That's right.

CASSIDY: I meant sex worker.

SERA: *(Standing up.)* I think it's time to start bringing out the main course. Cass, can I get some help?

*Shift scene to kitchen; CASSIDY and SERA prepare the food.*

CASSIDY: Shiiiiiiiiiiit! That girl is a moron and try-hard! You weren't exaggerating.

SERA: Put a lid on it.

CASSIDY: Come on! I'm just repeating what you said about her.

SERA: No, I mean put a lid on the green beans so they don't get cold. *(Pause.)* I just want us to have a nice dinner. Maybe I was harsh about Anaar. She's young.

CASSIDY: She's not that young.

SERA: Is this going to be a problem?

CASSIDY: No. I'll be cool. I just need to sit down and really enjoy my drink.

SERA: Wait, weren't you supposed to bring wine?

CASSIDY: I pay for everything with that app on my phone and –

SERA: You lost your phone. All right, okay, it's always something with you. Come on, we can't avoid them forever, and be nice.

CASSIDY: I thought I was!

*SERA and CASSIDY exit to the dining room where the conversation is in progress.*

ANAAR: You ran track?

SERA: No, n –

ANAAR: I meant Scott. You ran track? Me too!

SCOTT: Yeah? What'd you do?

ANAAR: Four hundred metre and long distance. You?

SCOTT: Eight hundred and sprints. You still run?

ANAAR: Every day.

SCOTT: Rain or shine?

ANAAR: Yup.

CASSIDY: Disciplined. Training for anything right now?

RUSHTON: She's not competitive.

CASSIDY: *(Breaking into Jamaican patois.)* Chuh, man! Let the gyal talk, man!

RUSHTON: Okay okay…I was just –

*CASSIDY cuts him off with a look.*

CASSIDY: G'head dahlin'.

ANAAR: Rushton's right. I'm not competitive. Not with other people. I like to see how far I can push myself, my body. But, I was thinking about doing the Stiletto Run this fall. It's for ovarian cancer research and I think it would be fun.

SCOTT: I'd do it!

ANAAR: There is a men's stiletto run too. Fifteen dollars to register and it's for a good cause.

SERA: You must be outta your goddamn minds! Pay to run in heels? So I can break my neck? Please. I could never do that. The only reason I'm running in heels is because I AM being chased.

ANAAR: Who'd be chasing you?

CASSIDY: Before we became teachers, me and Sera worked for Children's Aid.

ANAAR: Oh.

CASSIDY: You know what that means, right?

ANAAR: Kind of.

SERA: We were the ones who came to investigate you for allegations of child abuse, mistreatment, the works.

CASSIDY: If you saw me or Sera coming up your walkway you'd be shitting yourself. You don't want us on your doorstep. We're like cockroaches, cuz once we're in your house you can't get rid of us.

ANAAR: Damn!

SERA: If we're there, we've got cause. And no parent wants their kids taken away, no matter how feisty they are. I had to make a visit to a woman for slapping her fifteen-year-old daughter in the face for calling her a bitch. The kid called Children's Aid and I had to go. Now this was a Jamaican woman, you see. Black kids don't swear at their parents, at least they didn't when I was growing up. So, I leaned over and said to this mother, "Listen, if it was my kid I'd box her too, but this isn't the islands and you cyan't hit your kids. You just cyan't." Now, that's the parent that actually listened to me. The parents who don't listen, and I have to make a follow up visit? *(Kisses her teeth.)* I've been chased out of people's house, heels in hand, being called a fucking nigger so many times –

SCOTT: Sera, could we not use that word in the house?

CASSIDY: Uh oh.

SERA: Excuse me?

SCOTT: It makes me uncomfortable. I would rather –

SERA: YOU would rather? Huh, so are you telling me how to speak in my house?

SCOTT: No, that's not –

SERA: Wait a minute wait a minute here. Excuse me, guys. *(She turns to SCOTT.)* Let me get this straight: I'm not allowed –

SCOTT: I didn't say allowed –

SERA: Let me finish. You'd prefer if I not use the word, the n-word, if we're going to be polite here, in my, in our, house when referring to myself, in front of my friends because it makes you uncomfortable –

SCOTT: That's not –

SERA: Sweetie, I'm not finished. It makes you uncomfortable to hear that word used as I'm recounting a story where it was used against me by a racist redneck, but it's all right for you to use it when listening to Pac, NAS, Lil Wayne, Kanye, Jay-Z or any number of rap artists who use "nigger" in their songs?

ANAAR: Yeeah! Pac's my boy. "Livin' life as a thug nigga, until the day I die/Live the life as a boss playa / all eyes on me!"

*ANAAR starts rapping from "All Eyez on Me" until she's cut off by a look from CASSIDY and SERA.*

SCOTT: *(To SERA.)* Well, hon, I'm not trying to correct you but it's niggah, not nigger.

*Long pause.*

RUSHTON: You know what? I could really use a glass of water.

SERA: *(Sharply.)* You can wait. Scott, you did not just say that.

SCOTT: I'm sorry, I was trying to be funny. You're mad.

SERA: I'm not mad. I'm just trying to understand what just happened there.

SCOTT: Me too. I thought we were just having a conversation about running in heels and now this. I'm sorry, guys, I wasn't thinking. Maybe I've had too much wine.

SERA: No, no, I think this is something I'd like to ask you guys. I've grown up being called "nigger," "coon," "negro" even, for as long as I can remember, and now that one word has been appropriated, stolen, by so many people who should not be saying it. I'm guessing all of us, I mean, except my dear husband and Cassidy, have been called a nigger at least once in their lives.

ANAAR: I've never been called that word.

RUSHTON: Never?

ANAAR: No. Well, yes, uh...not by a stranger. My mom's family said it around me but not at me.

SERA: Around you but not at you?

ANAAR: They would call black people, um, THAT word when they didn't think that I was paying attention.

CASSIDY: What are you, anyway?

SERA: Cassidy!

ANAAR: No, it's fine, I get that a lot. People think I'm Indian, Spanish, Italian, a white girl with a tan.

SERA: And?

ANAAR: Lebanese/Jamaican.

CASSIDY: Me too!

ANAAR: You're Lebanese?

RUSHTON: News to me.

CASSIDY: No, I'm mixed. I'm Hakka-Chinese and Jamaican. Born in Kingston. My grandparents live next to a really nice Lebanese family in Mount Royal.

ANAAR: Ohhh…the food at your house must be sick!

CASSIDY: When I make the effort. So, what? You cyan't cook?

ANAAR: My mom did all the cooking and my dad left when I was really young. I never had West Indian food growing up so I have no idea how to make it.

CASSIDY: You poor ting.

ANAAR: I know! It's why I can't have ackee and saltfish waiting for Nana when he gets home after a long day at work.

SCOTT: Who's Nana?

RUSHTON: Oh, that's her pet name for me.

CASSIDY: Grandma? She calls you grandma?

ANAAR: No, it's short for banana.

SCOTT: I can't wait to hear this.

ANAAR: I used to do some modelling for art students at the university – well, sometimes nude, sometimes no, but anyway, I did it to make a little extra cash when I was waiting for bigger gigs. So, I'd get to the school early and wait in the cafeteria, read a magazine, whatever. Every day at the same time I'd see this guy walk in, buy a small milk and –

RUSHTON: A banana.

ANAAR: Perfect, no spots –

CASSIDY: *(To ANAAR.)* Just like you!

ANAAR: Thank you! I'd watch him do this every single week for months. He was like clockwork, right, babe? It would be 2:45, I'm in the caf, I'd have to be in the art room at 3:00, and in he'd walk, with that swagger of his, the smile; the women at the counter just loved him. I think they even saved the most perfect bananas just for him.

RUSHTON: *(Smugly.)* That's ridiculous. I don't remember it that way…

ANAAR: You remember what you want to remember. I had to see if I was right so one day I went up to the lunch counter, picked through the spotty fruit and asked if there were any without bruises and stuff and they said no. Then smoothie over here walks in, smiles that smile of his and gets handed perfection.

CASSIDY: You know that sometimes a perfect-looking banana can have a big brown gooey part, right? Or has that never happened to you?

RUSHTON: Never.

CASSIDY: Never?

RUSHTON: Nope.

CASSIDY: Appearances can be deceiving…just sayin'.

ANAAR: Anyway, one day came when the usual lunch ladies weren't there and all that was left were some pathetic-looking fruit. I watched him and he looked so disappointed that I went over, introduced myself and gave him, well, offered him, my perfect piece of fruit.

CASSIDY: There's a joke in there.

SCOTT: *(To CASSIDY.)* Nice.

ANAAR: And that's how we met.

RUSHTON: And you know, women love doctors the way girls love horses.

CASSIDY: Gross.

RUSHTON: I couldn't believe that a woman like this would give me the time of day. Just look at her. I mean, no wonder artists wanted to capture her in art.

ANAAR: It was just a still life class.

RUSHTON: Still life means bowls of fruit or an arrangement of flowers. Nudes, you mean nudes.

ANAAR: Oh.

RUSHTON: Speaking of flowers, my nickname for this one is inspired by them.

SERA: Which one?

ANAAR: Tulip…or broken tulip.

SERA: I'm sorry, what did you say?

RUSHTON: *(Warmly.)* My broken tulip. It's an interesting story, actually. In my research about botanical viruses, and such, I stumbled on an incredible, quite insightful article about Tulipmania in the 17th century.

SCOTT: Tulipmania? Like Beatlemania but for flowers?

RUSHTON: Exactly! Exactly right. In the 1600s, tulips became very popular in the Netherlands. It wasn't like anyone could grow tulips. At the time, it was a status symbol to be able to grow them. But the most popular and rare were called broken tulips because they were multi-coloured. A brown and white tulip or red with splashes of yellow… Anyway, these flowers caused a hysteria that was previously unseen in Dutch society. People wanted them so much that one bulb sold for ten thousand guilders, which was enough to buy a home in Amsterdam. People just lost their minds over these, these flowers! Of course, that kind of passion couldn't be sustained, especially when botanists discovered that it was a virus causing the tulips to break. Imagine that. The thing that was making it priceless was killing it.

CASSIDY: That's fucked.

RUSHTON: That's nature.

CASSIDY: No, it's fucked that you call your wife after a diseased flower.

RUSHTON: I think you're missing the point. I call her my broken tulip because she's invaluable, one of a kind…I'd sell everything, everything that I had to be with her, anything to make her happy.

CASSIDY: She's also mixed. Like the tulips. You're sick.

ANAAR: Biracial, I'd rather be called biracial.

CASSIDY: Biracial, half-breed, mulatto, mixed…it alllll the same ting.

RUSHTON: You're over-thinking it. Everyone loves flowers –

SERA: I don't.

*SCOTT blows a raspberry and gives a thumbs down.*

RUSHTON: The point is she is my beautiful tulip. I mean, look at her. Our kids are going to be gorgeous. You're just being contrary for the sake of it.

CASSIDY: And you're being obtuse to avoid an argument.

SCOTT: Can't you guys just say difficult and slow? We've all been to university.

RUSHTON: You need a boyfriend, Cass, because you're getting way too into this.

CASSIDY: I'll try not to blind myself with the rays of your self-congratulatory ego. Suck it, Rush.

RUSHTON: Meow. Would you like a saucer of milk?

SERA: Speaking of cats, Scott and I were thinking about getting a pet.

ANAAR: Get one of those cats from the toilet paper commercials. They're so cute!

SCOTT: Uh... a) they cost a shitload of money, b) I'm allergic, and c) the commercials are stupid. Pretty, fluffy white kittens to sell toilet paper? What am I supposed to think? That I want to wipe my ass with Snowball? It's fucked.

RUSHTON: How's work, anyway?

SCOTT: Brutal. When the economy is in the shitter the first thing companies want to cut is marketing. Companies with no sense of how the market works are hoping that viral marketing will save them. Social media is still the wild west with no rules. There's no way you can predict what's going to blow up. Someone has to be the voice of reason at the agency and I'm not sure if I'm it anymore. Man, I don't know how you do those lectures every day, fuck. I go into work every day hoping a client doesn't fire me. Or fall asleep during a pitch. Not necessarily in that order.

SERA: You're too hard on yourself.

RUSHTON: Or maybe he's not hard enough on himself.

SERA: Excuse me?

RUSHTON: This isn't university track and field. The only coach you have now is yourself.

CASSIDY: You're an inspiration poster for us all, Rush.

RUSHTON: Go ahead and make fun. I'm on track to make tenure, how's your career going, Cassidy?

ANAAR: I'd love one of those cats.

CASSIDY: Don't shame me about my choice of career. You only became a professor because you couldn't hack it in pharmaceuticals.

RUSHTON: Talking out of your ass again.

SCOTT: Let's keep it classy, could we?

CASSIDY: I'll bet you're an indifferent prof who just likes to hear himself talk.

ANAAR: I just think it would be nice to have a cat in the house to talk to once in a while.

SERA: You know getting a pet means you're preparing to have kids.

CASSIDY: Bullshit.

ANAAR: Yeah, what she said. *(Pointing her thumb to CASSIDY.)*

SERA: No, it's not. I can't tell you how many couples I know started with a puppy and a year later they had a baby.

CASSIDY: So what's my reason for getting a cat?

RUSHTON: You're an unmarried woman with no man. It's obvious.

CASSIDY: That's offensive and a predictably male thing to say. And what's so obvious?

ANAAR: That's not why I want a cat.

SCOTT: *(Laughing.)* Predictably male? Clarify that one for me, Cass.

CASSIDY: For reals guys, a single woman gets a pet and that automatically means she's lonely, but when a couple get a pet it's because they want a baby? You all don't believe that, do you? Can't a person just get a pet because they want a pet? What about the idea that couples have babies because they're lonely?

ANAAR: That's why I want one.

SERA: You're lonely?

RUSHTON: A baby?

ANAAR: A cat. And, no, I'm not lonely.

RUSHTON: We're not getting a cat.

ANAAR: Why not?

RUSHTON: We can't afford it.

ANAAR: *(Laughing.)* Very funny, we so can.

RUSHTON: Okay, you can't afford it. I'm not paying for a purebred Persian puss that will shed all over my clothes, scratch up my furniture and stink up my house. No cat.

CASSIDY: So, separate bank accounts, huh?

SERA: *(Hissing.)* Cassidy!

RUSHTON: *(Turning to SCOTT and SERA.)* You guys weren't thinking of getting a cat, were you? A nice Lab or even a pug would be great.

ANAAR: Seriously, babe?

CASSIDY: Do you even like women, Rushton?

RUSHTON: What? Listen, I hate cats! I'll be straight with you, I want us to get a puppy after my first baby is born. I think it would be nice for them to grow up together. I've seen couples have to give up a pet after their first kid was born because of incompatibility; like the cat gets jealous of the baby. Yeah, crazy shit like that. Also, toxoplasmosis can cause defects in the fetus if a woman is infected during pregnancy, especially in first pregnancies.

SERA: Anyone want more wine?

CASSIDY: Yes, please.

ANAAR: It's the kitty litter we have to be careful of so, you can change the litter. There. Fixed.

RUSHTON: I don't clean up cat shit. Anaar, it may sound harsh but it's for your own good. Trust me, sweetie, I'm a doctor. *(He kisses her.)*

SERA: Wow. Does that always work?

CASSIDY: They're still together, aren't they?

SCOTT: Speaking of sugar, is everyone ready for dessert?

CASSIDY: Anything to take the bad taste out of my mouth. What are we having?

SCOTT: Lemon chiffon.

CASSIDY: Homemade?

SCOTT: Well, it could have been but we ran out of butter so –

SERA: *(Warningly.)* Scott.

ANAAR: I need to pee. I'll be right back. Sera? This way or…?

SERA: Down the hall, past the armoire, to your left.

*ANAAR, a little tipsy, exits.*

SCOTT: Anyone want tea or coffee?

CASSIDY: Tea for me.

SERA: Me too.

RUSHTON: Pass.

*SCOTT exits.*

CASSIDY: She's lovely. The wife.

RUSHTON: You can't stand her.

CASSIDY: Not true. I think she's sweet and totally too good for you. Sera hates her.

SERA: I do not. Why would –

RUSHTON: You do?

SERA: Rush, can't you see what Cassidy is doing?

RUSHTON: No.

CASSIDY: Neither can I. Actually, she doesn't hate her.

SERA: Thank you, Cassidy.

CASSIDY: She just thinks she's a dumb-dumb.

SERA: No, I don't! Rushton, what does Anaar do, I mean, besides model, or act, or whatever?

RUSHTON: She's not modelling anymore. Didn't enjoy the travelling, the living out of a suitcase. Besides, she can afford not to work, but she's so stubborn and insists on making "her own money," as she puts it. I tell her my money is her money, but she keeps on working.

CASSIDY: Working at what?

RUSHTON: Avon.

SERA: What?

RUSHTON: She sells Avon.

SERA: People still do that?

RUSHTON: Yea.

CASSIDY: I love it. It's so retro. My mom used to sell Avon when she first immigrated here.

SERA: So did mine, but then she got a job. I don't know how she does it, I could never do that.

RUSHTON: You're both snobs, you know that, right?

CASSIDY: I wonder if they still sell Skin-So-Soft. I heard it helps keep mosquitoes away. Might come in handy for when I go camping. Remind me to ask her when she gets back.

SERA: You don't camp.

CASSIDY: Maybe I will now. Smellin' good and West Nile free.

*ANAAR re-enters.*

SERA: *(Laughing.)* Jamaicans don't camp.

ANAAR: I love the Jamaican theme in the bathroom, Sera.

SERA: Thanks, but it was Scott who came up with the design of the bathroom. He saw the palm tree shower curtain and was inspired.

ANAAR: It's pretty.

SERA: Anaar, what does your name mean? It's so unusual.

ANAAR: It means grenade in French.

SERA: Really?

CASSIDY: Interesting.

*SCOTT enters holding mugs.*

ANAAR: Oh! And congratulations!

SERA: On what?

ANAAR: The baby! When I first saw you tonight and you weren't drinking I thought, "Is she?" but then I saw the test in the bathroom. Congratulations!

SCOTT: You opened our medicine cabinet?

RUSHTON: You're pregnant?

*Long pause.*

SERA: No.

*Sound of birds taking flight and SERA is featured in a spotlight.*

In life there's the before and the after. Sometimes you have a child and then you don't. I never thought about this before, until I went to check in on one of the kids I was monitoring for my job. She was a little thing with parents who were overwhelmed. They called her Piaf, not like the singer, but like the bird. Did you know "piaf" means "sparrow" in French? She had a big smile that took up most of her face and this little girl, wooo, she liked to sing. Badly, but at least she tried, you know? Drove her parents crazy with her singing every morning before school, but one day they realized that something was missing in their house at 7 am. And they go into her room and she's still in bed. And she is blue. She has died. Sometime that morning their eight-year-old baby girl has had a heart attack. A heart attack… and…stupid, the stupid things you think when you're hit with something traumatic. I think, "But she wasn't overweight, she wasn't under stress, she didn't smoke she wasn't…" And by this point I'm crying. I, my eyes are filled and, and, my breath is constricted because their sparrow has died and they were NOT PREPARED. I was not prepared and she wasn't even my baby… I felt my heart, it was beating but, really, really slowly, not making much of a sound because it was squeezing my rib cage. That doesn't even make any sense but…that's what it felt like. Like I couldn't breathe. Like I had no control. And you know what? None of us have any control. Not at all. That's what I know now. I lost this fifth baby. Lost? I had a miscarriage! My fifth. Just fell out of me. So much blood. Poor Scott. Poor sweet Scott…. Only this time, this time I believed that it was going to happen. I was going to be a mother. "I'm going to have a baby," I thought. I thought, "Why would God give me a fifth and then take it away?" Again. It's not possible. That – this, CAN NOT happen to me. Again. Me. I care about kids, other people's kids, I go to the gym every day, I, I, I. I did everything right. But then I remember the time I snapped at the autistic kid in my class, I remember I was pissed about the morning sickness that lasted all day long and I had a tiny, tiny, mmm awful thought that maybe I wasn't meant to be a mom, it was a glimpse of a thought!

And that's when he got me. Poof. You got your wish, Sera. Whatever will be will be and I lost her. Five months. Shouldn't have kept her a secret, I guess. I dunno. Secrets always find a way of flying out and you can't catch them. I just thought that if I said anything I'd, you know, superstitious West Indian… But I was wrong. Here we are. No baby. Her name was going to be Ava, after my mom. I probably shouldn't have given her a name but… Did I mention it was a girl?

ANAAR: Um…what's going on?

CASSIDY: Boom.

SCOTT: Get out. All of you. Out. *(Pause.)* You were right, Sera. She is a moron.

# Act Two

## Scene 1

*Dark stage except for a spotlight on ANAAR, sleeping in bed. The soundscape is of rain or a brook over-layered with the birdsong of the black-capped chickadee. A Gregory Crewdson photo come to life. She wakes with a start and sits up in bed.*

ANAAR: Rushton, I just had a dream that I was walking down a busy street in a long white nightgown, I crossed a bridge that led to a beautiful house that was made of glass and chrome. When I walked in there was a pool, a shallow pool filled with silvery fish that jumped up and settled right here. *(She rests her hand on her abdomen.)* It was so real, Rushton, so so…umm vivid. The room, I think it was the living room, was filled with light, a sparkly multicoloured light, and I could see outside that the house was surrounded by clean, clear water that was also filled with these tiny, shiny fish. I walked into my room, because I knew it was my room, and sat on the bed and went to sleep. Imagine that…a dream about sleeping…. when I woke up the bedroom door cracked open and a thousand paper cranes flew in and filled the room. And then…and then you were there! You looked so handsome…so strong and you came over, kissed me long and hard and as you pulled away a dove flew out of my mouth. I closed my eyes for just a second and you were gone. It was… beautiful but I just knew you were gone. You left me. Please don't leave me, Rushton. Please don't go.

*Parrot tulip petals rain from the sky as the lights go down.*

## Scene 2

*ANAAR and RUSHTON's bedroom. ANAAR is in bed and RUSHTON is standing, looking out the window.*

ANAAR: You're going to have to start talking to me eventually. *(Long pause.)* It's been two days of this. I'm not apologizing anymore. I'm done.

RUSHTON: You're done when you mean it.

ANAAR: I do mean it.

RUSHTON: Do you even know what you're apologizing for or why?

ANAAR: –

RUSHTON: What were you thinking?

ANAAR: What's the big deal? I mean I get it, but who keeps a pregnancy test after…

RUSHTON: That's not the point! Were you at least looking for something in particular?

ANAAR: No. I think it's interesting to look through people's stuff. I've been doing it for…. I dunno. I mean, I can't even remember when I started. It's like finding a secret that you're not supposed to. Does that make sense?

RUSHTON: –

ANAAR: Let me make you a tuna fish sandwich. You're just hungry. I haven't seen you eat at all these past few days.

RUSHTON: I eat at work. And it's tuna, not tuna fish. A tuna sandwich. You wouldn't say chicken poultry sandwich, would you? Or tortellini pasta salad? Would you? It's redundant.

ANAAR: Okay, I get it, you're smarter than me. There's no reason to be an asshole. I'm sorry I upset your friend, all right? It's not like you're her husband or her best friend. I had too much to drink and I wasn't thinking. Why can't you just see that and let it go?

RUSHTON: Because no woman who has any sense about having kids or wanting them or, fuck, even a woman who has female friends would announce somebody else's pregnancy. And why were you going through their medicine cabinet? Who does that?

ANAAR: Everybody does that!

RUSHTON: No, they don't! It's rude and an invasion of privacy.

ANAAR: If you don't want people going through your stuff, then lock it.

RUSHTON: You've got to be kidding.

ANAAR: People are naturally curious and I guess I just –

RUSHTON: Oh, so you're a social anthropologist now?

ANAAR: Jesus!

RUSHTON: Tell me something. Weren't you a little curious about the fact that they hadn't said anything about being pregnant and maybe they didn't want to?

ANAAR: No.

RUSHTON: No? It didn't occur to you that maybe Sera wanted to wait to say anything since maybe it was too early to say anything?

ANAAR: No.

RUSHTON: It just seems that you're tone deaf to the kids thing, you know? Mentioning the baby at the dinner party, not thinking about the reasons for why you shouldn't have said anything, not calling to apologize to Sera… I've talked about wanting kids and you've been lukewarm at best. I feel like I'm the one who's always talking about it and it just occurred to me that you've never actually said, "Yes, I want kids." Do you?

ANAAR: –

RUSHTON: Do you want kids, Anaar? Do want to have children? With me?

*Long pause.*

ANAAR: I don't think everyone is meant to be a parent. I mean, don't you think that Sera and Scott are just forcing it? They've been married forever and trying for years and still no babies. Maybe they should take it as a sign that it's not meant to be.

RUSHTON: Wait, so if it doesn't happen naturally, people should just forget it?

ANAAR: Maybe. Yes.

RUSHTON: I can't believe we've never talked about this. I can't believe you don't want kids. What was I thinking?

ANAAR: I never said that. You never ever asked me. It was just assumed that we would have them.

RUSHTON: But you never said you didn't want them!

ANAAR: You never asked me!

RUSHTON: Well, I'm asking you now. Anaar, do you want kids? Yes or no.

ANAAR: Did you ever think that maybe you're asking the wrong question?

RUSHTON: Stop pivoting!

ANAAR: What does that mean?

RUSHTON: I feel like I'm talking to a fucking politician. Do you want kids?

ANAAR: I can't. I'm unable to have children.

RUSHTON: What do you mean, you're unable?

ANAAR: I mean I have a condition that makes it impossible.

RUSHTON: You're infertile?

ANAAR: I was born with a condition called Complete Androgen Insensitivity Syndrome.

RUSHTON: Androgen…that means –

ANAAR: You're an expert with viruses, but I'm pretty sure you haven't heard of this. This is gender-related.

RUSHTON: Not gynecological?

ANAAR: No. This is hard to talk about and I know I should have told you a long time ago. Maybe even on our second date, but you were so great and we hit it off so well that I didn't know how to bring it up. I figured, maybe this wouldn't work out and I'd never have to tell you. That's what's happened with all my other relationships. They'd peter out and I never had to tell them anything about my… medical "issues." But with you…it just kept working.

RUSHTON: Mmmhm.

ANAAR: With you everything just worked. I didn't feel like I had to try so hard because we clicked, you know? I kept thinking that at some point the whole kids thing would just go away. I thought that once you realized that pregnancy wasn't happening, for whatever reason, you'd accept that we weren't going to be parents and love me anyway. Is that crazy?

RUSHTON: You know for sure that it's not possible? I've talked to Scott about this –

ANAAR: About us?

RUSHTON: Well, not directly, but I have had conversations with him about what he and Sera have gone through and the topic of IVF has come up.

ANAAR: No.

RUSHTON: Wait. Hear me out. Infertility is a serious medical condition. One in six couples here experience infertility and IVF treatments are covered by the government. If that's what we're dealing with, and believe me when I say "we," because this is something you and I will deal with together. I wish you'd felt comfortable enough to tell me this earlier. I love you and I will be by your side as we go through this.

ANAAR: *(Big sigh.)* This is a lot more complicated than getting IVF.

RUSHTON: What do you mean, more complicated?

ANAAR: I'm not like other…women. I can't have children because I was never born with a uterus or fallopian tubes. There are no ovaries in here and that obviously means no eggs. I realized there was something wrong with me when everyone in school had their period but me. I also noticed that all the girls in my gym class had a lot more pubic hair than me and shaved their pits, which I didn't have to do. It was just me and my mom by then, and even though we never talked about sex or my body, I knew I had to talk to her about taking me to the doctor. I was found to have internal testes and no female reproductive system, which is called CAIS or complete androgen insensitivity syndrome.

RUSHTON: Internal testes…? Are you a hermaphrodite?

ANAAR: No! And hermaphrodite is terrible term, by the way. I'm a girl, a woman. I just wasn't born with everything. I had the testes removed because they were in my abdomen and could have become cancerous.

RUSHTON: I thought you said that scar was from an accident.

ANAAR: I lied.

RUSHTON: Yeah, it sounds like you lied about a lot of things.

ANAAR: What was I supposed to say? "Oh, that? That's my orchidectomy scar, because even though I look, smell, and fuck like a woman, I'm genetically a man and was born with internal testes."

RUSHTON: You've been pretending to be something you're not for years with me! What have you been doing with the tampons I've been buying for you? Since you can't and don't have a period, have you just been throwing them out? Have you actually had cramps? Needed to take Advil for the pain?

ANAAR: No.

RUSHTON: Wait, I've seen you take the pill! I mean, I've picked up your prescription, so I can't believe you went through all that to fool me. Is that what you've been doing? Well, I guess if you could fool this doctor you could fool one into writing you a script for birth control. Wow, just wow!

ANAAR: I do take the pill because I need it for the estrogen. My body doesn't produce enough and that's why I had to get these. *(She gestures at her breasts.)* I know I said it was for modelling, but –

RUSHTON: Lies, lies, lies…

ANAAR: Stop saying that! I did not lie to you.

RUSHTON: A lie by omission is still a lie.

ANAAR: I don't know what that means.

RUSHTON: It means leaving shit out, Anaar. It means telling some, but not all, of the truth to suit your purposes.

ANAAR: And you've never done that? You've been completely honest with me? All of the time? Everybody lies.

RUSHTON: Not me.

ANAAR: Liar. I saw how you fawned over Sera, is that a crush?

RUSHTON: So, you're jealous now.

ANAAR: And the way you and Cassidy fight, she's totally got a thing for you.

RUSHTON: *(Laughs.)* Uh no, she was my ex from high school and hasn't grown up much since then.

ANAAR: Your ex?! Is that one of your lying by omission deals you were talking about?

RUSHTON: This conversation isn't about me. It's about whatever "this" is, this, this relationship.

ANAAR: A relationship is two people! Stop putting the blame on me, only me. You act like I've had a say in what we do in this marriage, but you took control and expected me to just go along. Where we lived, where we went on vacation, whether we got a pet. Hey, now that there won't be a baby, can we get the cat that I wanted? Silly question, I know the answer is no, because we, I mean, I can't afford it.

RUSHTON: Don't be cute. You don't make any money. Selling Avon products isn't a career and we both know that.

ANAAR: Fine. Then I'll quit and do something else.

RUSHTON: That seems to be what you're good at, isn't it? Quitting. You quit school, you quit modelling, you couldn't quite make it as an actress. Yeah, I said *actress* because, let's be honest, since we're on a streak here of telling the truth, the only acting you seemed to get involved in required selling more than your personality. You didn't think I knew about those videos, did you? But I would have to say the one thing you've proven to be good at is running; running away from yourself and your problems, your family, just like your father.

ANAAR: You can stop now.

RUSHTON: Apple doesn't fall too far, huh?

ANAAR: You've made your point.

RUSHTON: Really? And what is my point?

ANAAR: –

RUSHTON: What is my point?

ANAAR: I don't even know any more.

*RUSHTON walks over to the bed and kneels on the floor beside ANAAR and takes her hands.*

RUSHTON: I know it seems like I'm being cruel, but I just need you to see how much you've hurt me with your lies. Actions have consequences. I wanted to have a family with you, the most beautiful woman I've ever met. That's the first thing I thought when I saw you. Babies. My babies with this…this gorgeous creature will be my future.

ANAAR: And that's it, isn't it? You looked at me and all you could think about was what you could get out of me –

RUSHTON: No, that's –

ANAAR: *(Pulling her hands away.)* Stop touching me. Let me finish. You looked at me and you thought of how I would make you look. Not about me. You didn't think about me. Oh, I like being called beautiful, but is that all you see? Do you think… *(Takes a deep breath.)* Am I smart or interesting to you? Or even your equal?

RUSHTON: My equal? We're partners, Anaar! I married you because I loved you.

ANAAR: I feel like you wanted to slot me into the perfect picture of the life you thought you should have. Perfect job, perfect wife, and now you need the baby to make the picture complete. But now that it's not quite what you expected, you can't fix this…what now?

RUSHTON: We could adopt or hire a surrogate.

ANAAR: Rush, do I seem maternal to you? Have you ever seen me coo over a baby or stop to smell their heads the way you do? *(Pause.)* I'd like to take care of you and maybe a pet, even a dog if you like. Is that still on the table?

*RUSHTON stands up and walks away.*

RUSHTON: I want to be a father.

ANAAR: Why?

RUSHTON: I just do. How do you know you won't feel maternal if we brought a child home?

ANAAR: I just do. I've spent a big part of my life knowing that I couldn't have children. And maybe knowing that you absolutely can't have something makes it easier to deal with and I've dealt with it. I am telling you right now: I don't want to be anyone's mommy.

RUSHTON: Well, I'm just dealing with it now so I'm going to need some time. This is news to me as of – now! I need a break.

*RUSHTON walks out of the room.*

ANAAR: I thought we were trying to have a conversation! RUSHTON! RUSHTON!!

*The sound of a door slams, petals fall from the flowers in the vase. ANAAR stays in bed for a moment before dragging herself out and to the master bathroom offstage, taking the vase with her.*

## Scene 3

*Later in the day. SCOTT is in his home gym stretching and the music is loud. RUSHTON enters just as SCOTT is about to start his circuit. SCOTT does not stop working out throughout the entire scene except when he speaks to RUSHTON at the end.*

RUSHTON: Hey.

SCOTT: Hey Rush, what's up?

RUSHTON: Sera let me in so…

SCOTT: Give me a hand here?

RUSHTON: Yeah, sure. (*Pauses as he kneels down to hold SCOTT's feet as he does sit-ups.*) This is quite a setup you have here. I don't think I've ever been down in the, in your church of…modern fitness. I mean, it's impressive, no wonder you look so good. So strong. I've been tempted, man, I've been tempted to go to the school gym, you know? I don't have to pay for it because, well, you know, but I just never get around to it. I thought about getting a few weights and an elliptical or treadmill at the condo but I just know I'd get home from work and be too tired or too busy grading papers to even change into track pants. I thought about working out at lunch time, but that's when I have office hours…for my students to come see me, right. I mean, what kind of professor would I be if they couldn't reach me because I was at the gym or going for a run, not that I run. That's Anaar's thing.

*There is a long pause, during which SERA enters unseen and hides behind the doorframe.*

Anaar, yeah, about that, that thing that happened and what she did, I just wanted to say that I'm sorry, man. I don't know what she was thinking and I – I – talked to her. I talked to her about it and she – I don't know, Scott. I just don't know who I married. You're lucky. You met Sera in high school so you got to grow up together and it was easier for you two. Well, I don't mean easier –

SCOTT: What are you talking about, Rush?

RUSHTON: I wanted to apologize.

SCOTT: For what?

RUSHTON: For Anaar. What happened was –

SCOTT: Don't worry about it. I'm sorry I called her a moron.

RUSHTON: But the thing is that…night…well, Anaar and I got to talking and, she doesn't want kids, Scott. Actually, she can't have them, not at all.

SCOTT: Sorry, man. I can give you the name of the people we've been using if –

RUSHTON: No, Scott. She is physically unable to have children.

SCOTT: Huh. Well…and she doesn't want to adopt?

RUSHTON: No.

SCOTT: In sickness and in health, buddy.

RUSHTON: So, I'm supposed to just take this? She lies to me and I'm supposed to say, oh well, I guess we'll get a pet, like that's some kind of substitute?

SCOTT: Take it? I understand that you're upset, but what about her? She can't have kids and you're acting like the slighted boyfriend? Do you have any idea how she even feels about this, how she felt when she found out that she was, what, infertile? Is that what it is?

RUSHTON: It's more complicated than that.

SCOTT: You know what? I don't want to know.

RUSHTON: Why are you getting so pissed at me? I've been your friend for over twenty years. You barely know my wife.

SCOTT: Do you know how many times Sera and I have had to get a new mattress in the last five years? Two. Two times, Rushton, and do you want to know why? Because miscarriages are messy. There's so much blood you can't look at anything else. You get the blood in your clothes and you smell it in the room long after the mattress is gone. In the movies, there's the shot of a woman groaning a little, clutching her abdomen and then they cut away. What actually happens when a thirty-eight-year-old woman miscarries her fifth child is horrifying and it stays with you forever. I don't sleep, I sometimes can't touch my wife because I don't want to cause her that kind of suffering again because it keeps happening. "In sickness and in health" are not just words, they're a promise. And I don't need to be your wife's best friend to know that she's probably going through a personal hell. What I don't understand is why you can't see past your own ego to recognize that.

RUSHTON: I want kids.

SCOTT: I, I, I…and if Anaar can't make that happen, then what? Not all of us are meant to be parents, Rushton.

RUSHTON: You and Sera keep trying.

SCOTT: And we won't stop until she says so. I owe her that.

RUSHTON: And what about you? What do you deserve?

SCOTT: I got what I deserve. A woman who loves me, a job that I may or may not still have and the possibility, however faint, to be a father one day.

RUSHTON: That's what you want? But what do you need?

SCOTT: Wants and needs…tricky things. You wanted a beautiful wife, you wanted a great job, you want a baby. Do you need any of these things? Would you be happy with an all-right-looking woman who could give you kids over a stunner who can't? You have a position at the university, but if it meant more time with your non-existent kids in the future, would you get a low-profile job in a lab? It's all about choices. It's about being faithful to your own truths.

RUSHTON: What is truth? I mean really?

*SCOTT is silent and works out more.*

All right. Okay. I'm going. I have to think this through. I'll holler at ya in some time, 'kay?

SCOTT: You treat her like a trophy and you're surprised that she has no depth.

RUSHTON: What did you say?

SCOTT: At dinner. It was all about how beautiful she was and what gorgeous children you were going to have and at no point did it appear, to me anyway, that you were interested in her at all. It was the appearances that seemed to concern you.

RUSHTON: Where is this coming from? What gives you the right to –

SCOTT: You're right, Rush, I am one of your oldest friends and I'm calling it as it is, since it appears that you're getting ready to bail. Or not. Maybe you're going to surprise me here. But the Rushton I grew up with treated women like shit.

RUSHTON: I love women. I love my wife. I used to be an asshole, but none of us were saints, except you, of course.

SCOTT: I'm not saying I was saint or that I'm better than you.

RUSHTON: Really?

SCOTT: Don't let Sera's act fool you. She knows me and still stays. *That* woman is a saint. When I was in the States I knew I could never get caught. I took advantage of all that freedom and no, Sera and I did not have an agreement. If the roles were reversed I would never put up with other guys, so I was an asshole. I know that I have that in me. I see what you have in you and it can't take you far in relationships, Rush. The trouble is you're still convinced that the world owes you something because you're a smart, good-looking black man. You didn't end up in jail or on the streets or dead, so you take what you believe you deserve.

RUSHTON: Where the hell did you get this bullshit?

SCOTT: Tell me the truth. Are you thinking of ending it with Anaar right now?

RUSHTON: I don't have to answer to you for anything, especially what happens in my marriage.

*RUSHTON begins to leave.*

SCOTT: I got someone pregnant when I was on scholarship.

*RUSHTON stops and SERA slips away unseen.*

I was eighteen, hot shit, and the girls were unbelievable. Anyone else would have caved long before I did. That's how I justified fucking around. For me it was "what happens in Texas stays in Texas," because I knew none of my boys on the team were going to say anything to anyone. Hell, they had their own girls to deal with and I was from Canada, man. Goody goody, no-shit-on-our-hands Canada. None of the girls I messed with could even find it on a map so I wasn't worried they would find me after.

RUSHTON: You have a kid out there?

SCOTT: I have a son.

RUSHTON: And Sera doesn't know?

SCOTT: No. I don't think she would leave me over it, but the knowledge of a child, a child that's mine and not hers, out there somewhere would really hurt her. I couldn't do that to her.

RUSHTON: So she's never going to know and you'll spend the rest of your life paying penance?

SCOTT: Not all truths need to be told and I don't think loving my wife too much is paying penance.

RUSHTON: You think lying to her is loving her too much… interesting. I'm pretty sure that's what Anaar was thinking when she lied to me. But I believe you need to have faith that the facts won't kill the love that exists between you. It sounds like you don't trust Sera to handle something that she may be strong enough to take.

SCOTT: I think I know my wife, thank you. She is more than strong enough, but why give her one more burden to carry? You know the truth about your wife now. Are you man enough to deal with it? Do you wish you'd never found out?

RUSHTON: You know, I had a conversation with a student about Joan of Arc years ago that I've never forgotten. I told him that scientists had a theory that the voices Joan heard were not God speaking through Archangel Michael but paranoid schizophrenia. This guy lost it. "Why can't people just leave it be? Why do scientists have to diagnose every fucking thing? She heard voices and it was the voice of God. She sought victory for France, she won, and the explanation is she was crazy? That's bullshit." Back then I thought that sometimes the truth is some bitter medicine that you have to choke down. After all, I am a scientist and it's my job to sort through the messy details.

SCOTT: And now?

RUSHTON: It's very different to be on the other side. I wonder if it would've been better if I'd never found out the truth about Anaar. *(Pause and a big sigh.)*

SCOTT: Nobody teaches us how to deal with shit like this. Call me if you want to come over, talk, or watch the game.

RUSHTON: Yeah. *(He turns to leave.)*

SCOTT: And Rush, I'm really not trying to be an asshole.

RUSHTON: Yeah, man, I know.

*RUSHTON exits.*

## Scene 4

*SERA and SCOTT's place, in the kitchen. CASSIDY is there with SERA. There are unpacked bags of groceries on the counter and floor.*

CASSIDY: I need your phone number.

SERA: Had to get a new cell, huh?

CASSIDY: I'm $800 in the hole. I have to re-enter all my contacts. Technology is bankrupting us all while making us completely dependent on it. I miss the 80s.

SERA: It just seemed simpler in the 80s. Back then we were worried about the Cold War, remember?

CASSIDY: Oh yeah…Sting had that great song about whether Russians loved their children, too.

*There's an awkward silence.*

You know, Rushton was sort of right.

SERA: About what?

CASSIDY: Why I want a cat.

SERA: You've been talking about getting a cat for years, don't listen to Rushton. He's just trying to get under your skin.

CASSIDY: It worked. Remember in Grade Ten when we had that Kiwanis trip and I had a little breakdown in the van?

SERA: Oh yeah! It was scary. You were crying and hysterical. You kept saying, "I left the apples on the table" over and over again because you were supposed to bring the fruit for the trip.

CASSIDY: I was convinced that we were all going to die in that van and then my mom would come home from work, see that I was stealing apples for you guys and be pissed. But of course we would be dead after swerving to avoid hitting a deer and my mom would feel guilty for being mad at me.

SERA: THAT's what you were crying about?

CASSIDY: If I died today I'd have nothing left behind. Not even a bag of apples.

SERA: What are you talking about, Cass?

CASSIDY: I don't have a legacy, Sera. I'm single, no kids, and running out of time to have any if I wanted… and I don't know if I do. If Scott died today at least he has you to carry on his memory. Even Anaar has paintings that commemorate her existence and she's a flake. Rushton has his extensive research and patents carrying his name and what do I have? Nothing. If I died today nobody would know.

SERA: Not true.

CASSIDY: You take it for granted that you have someone to talk to when you get home. You would be so missed if you died.

SERA: You would be missed, Cassidy, don't be ridiculous.

CASSIDY: Did you see the story about that British woman who died in her apartment and wasn't found for three years?

SERA: Please.

CASSIDY: No, it's true. The woman was sitting in front of her TV THAT WAS STILL ON, surrounded by Christmas presents that she was wrapping. Three years.

SERA: She was old though, right?

CASSIDY: Thirty-eight years old.

SERA: That won't happen to you.

CASSIDY: How do you know?

SERA: I'm offended.

CASSIDY: You're offended?

SERA: Cassidy, I would never let three years go by without a phone call, a text or an email. And neither would your mother.

CASSIDY: What if she died before me?

SERA: Come on, Cassidy! Stop it.

CASSIDY: I'm afraid I'm going to die alone and no one would miss me.

SERA: You could still have a kid. You're thirty-eight, you've got time.

CASSIDY: Remember when Murphy Brown had a baby?

SERA: Are you talking about the TV show?

CASSIDY: Yeah, well, I remember watching the episode and she's singing "You Make Me Feel Like a Natural Woman" to her new baby in the hospital room and I just knew: I'm never having kids and that's okay.

SERA: So when you thought you were pregnant in high school and then found out you weren't –

CASSIDY: It was confusing, since nobody wants to be pregnant in high school, but I figured it might be a way to keep my boyfriend. Teenagers can be so stupid...can you imagine if I'd had a kid at sixteen?

SERA: Your mother would have disowned you and we probably wouldn't be friends now.

CASSIDY: Seriously.

SERA: Seriously. Cassidy Lam, you're not going to die alone. And you're nothing like that woman in England. If you're serious about getting a cat, we can take a trip to the shelters this weekend.

CASSIDY: I love you, Sera Hansa.

SERA: You're going to be fine. You may not see it, but you have more freedom than a lot of people. No husband, no kids…

CASSIDY: About that, how are you?

SERA: I don't feel like talking about it right now, Cassidy.

*Long pause.*

I'm fine. I have good days and not-so-good days.

CASSIDY: You can always, always talk to me.

SERA: How about this, when you see a rainbow in the sky, call. Those can be some of the worse days for me.

CASSIDY: Why?

SERA: *(Shakes her head.)* Just call.

*CASSIDY takes SERA's hand.*

CASSIDY: I think I'm going to start online dating again.

SERA: I hear there's a wealth of serial killers and fraudsters on those sites. Knock yourself out.

CASSIDY: Hey! I know a friend of a friend's cousin who met her husband on one of those sites.

SERA: Which one?

CASSIDY: AshleyMadison.

SERA: And she's still married to him? Girl, it is rough out there. I'm praying for you. Coffee? It's a new blend I picked up.

*SERA picks up the pot to pour herself a cup.*

CASSIDY: Can't. I just went to the dentist and my mouth still feels hurty.

SERA: Cavity?

CASSIDY: Nah. Half of my tooth fell out last night while I was on a date. Not online this time.

SERA: How'd you meet?

CASSIDY: I was riding my bike and this not-bad-looking cop –

SERA: He's a cop?

CASSIDY: A bike cop! I'm standing there trying to find a place to lock up my bike when this bike cop comes up and says, "If you lock it up over there, I'll keep an eye on it with my buddy," and points to another cop rolling up behind him. I'm like, all right, I got the cops on my side, so I say sure. I just needed to run into a store and get something. So of course it takes longer than it's supposed to and by the time I get out of the store no more po-po. He's gone and I'm like, whatever. All of a sudden he drives up beside me in a black, tricked-out jeep and he's like, "What took you so long? I waited as long as I could but my shift's over so I'm heading home now." Long story short, he gave me his number and we went on a date.

SERA: I didn't know that stuff happened in real life.

CASSIDY: It gets better. So we meet at a nice enough place and he's already sitting in a booth when I get there: he has a skullet, Sera.

SERA: What's a skullet?

CASSIDY: Balding in the front and a teeny tiny ponytail in the back.

SERA: What the frick makes a man think that's a good idea?

CASSIDY: Girls dig a man with a ponytail.

SERA: In 1972, maybe. When a nude Burt Reynolds on a bearskin rug seemed like a good idea but ugh, that sounds wrong. Didn't you know he was bald when he gave you his number?

CASSIDY: First of all, not bald, skullet. And second, he was wearing a bike helmet when we met.

SERA: He was off duty and in his jeep when he asked you out.

CASSIDY: And wearing a baseball hat. Can I finish?

SERA: Please.

CASSIDY: Besides, I think bald men are pretty hot, all that testosterone, right? But the wispy bit being held back by a pink elastic this guy is rocking is turning me off. So, I think to myself, give him a chance, maybe his personality will make up for it.

SERA: And?

CASSIDY: He kept referring to himself in the third person and would actually say, "LOL," you know, for "laugh out loud." If I've said it once I'll say it again, Faceboob has made people into fucking morons. So, I'm trying to think of a good reason to ditch this loser when he says he has to hit the head. Classy, very classy. He hops down. HOPS! From the booth because he's probably no taller than 5'3."

SERA: You're tiny, too.

CASSIDY: Yeah, but I am taller than him. No dice, can't do it. And then like a cherry on a sundae he pulls out a huge wad of cash held with another pink elastic, pulls out a few bills, and tells me to order him another rusty nail.

SERA: So you bailed when he went to the bathroom?

CASSIDY: No, that would be rude! But my tooth fell out, well, half of it did, when he was in the bathroom and that gave me a legitimate excuse to bounce.

SERA: How does that happen?

CASSIDY: The bad date?

SERA: No, a piece of your tooth falling out?

CASSIDY: I'm no longer covered by my parents' insurance, so I haven't been to a dentist in fifteen years.

SERA: Come on!

CASSIDY: Dentists are like doctors. I think they're all witches.

SERA: I can't believe you have a university degree.

CASSIDY: They don't know what they're talking about half the time. It's all guesswork and western voodoo.

SERA: Smile at me.

*CASSIDY grins widely.*

You have really nice teeth.

CASSIDY: I do. Except the one that fell out. I don't need dentists. Sera, I go to sleep with candy in my mouth.

SERA: Well, now that you're back on the market, maybe you should give Rushton a call.

CASSIDY: What happened to the try-hard?

SERA: She's not so bad, Cass.

CASSIDY: Tell me you don't look at her and see one of those chicks trying to steal your man back in high-school?! *(Kisses her teeth.)* Besides, I'd never date Rushton again. High school was enough and remember, you can't cross the same river twice.

SERA: She came over here to apologize to me about what happened at dinner. I guess things got rocky between the two of them after.

CASSIDY: I thought she was his perfect little tulip.

SERA: She can't have kids.

CASSIDY: What's wrong with her?

SERA: There's nothing wrong with her. She doesn't have anything down here. *(Gesturing to the abdominal area.)* No uterus or anything. I probably shouldn't be telling you this but –

CASSIDY: Wait wait wait…so her coochie is –

SERA: – like a cul-de-sac rather than a winding road.

CASSIDY: That's bizarre.

SERA: It's sad, Cassidy, and it's not fair. She never told Rush, he started pressuring her for kids, she told him about her condition and poof, it's over.

CASSIDY: He dumped her. What a tool. Okay, now I feel bad for her. It may have happened over twenty years ago, but I haven't forgotten that he ditched me when he thought I was pregnant.

SERA: Yes, but you told him your parents would never let you keep it because it would be a mixed-up Chinee black pickney. Nobody had clean hands back then.

CASSIDY: Okay, true, but your boyfriend should stand by you no matter what and he failed that test. He used to talk about how great it would be when we got married and had those kids. And then when I told him I might be preggers, he dropped me.

*SCOTT enters.*

Hi honey.

SCOTT: Hey love.

*SCOTT kisses CASSIDY and then his wife.*

CASSIDY: If only Rushton could have been more like you.

SCOTT: Thanks!

SERA: He ain't perfect, and you know what, Cassidy? It's been twenty years. It's time to let it go. "He who covers and forgives an offense seeks love, but he who repeats or harps on a matter separates even close friends."

CASSIDY: *(Stares at SERA for a moment.)* Okay. Listen, I gotta go. I need more painkillers for my chompers and prayers won't help. Ciao!

*CASSIDY grabs the bag of coffee beans surreptitiously as she exits.*

SCOTT: Painkillers?

SERA: Half a tooth broke off in the middle of her date with a bike cop who had a skullet.

SCOTT: There's a story in there somewhere. Do I want to hear it?

SERA: Maybe later. *(She picks up the newspaper on the table*). Remember that case I worked on a few years ago where a baby was found in a stairwell?

SCOTT: Mmm... Vaguely. Remind me. *(He begins unpacking the groceries.)*

SERA: A baby was found face-down at the bottom of some stairs in a parking garage. I was still with Children's Aid then and I remember thinking that it had to be a teen mother that did it.

SCOTT: You didn't talk about it much.

SERA: I wasn't allowed to talk about it. Cases like that have to be kept quiet.

SCOTT: You quit after that case, right?

SERA: Yeah well, I'm glad I did. Look at this.

*SERA shows SCOTT a story in the paper which he scans quickly.*

SCOTT: Unbelievable.

SERA: It's the same people from a few years ago. You know they had three other kids that we found who were sick and starving. And the parents, if you can even call them that, paid a $300 fine and got a slap on the wrist. And now this. They run and hide in Jamaica but the devil finds work for idle hands, another dead child, and in a suitcase no less.

SCOTT: You're not saying this is the work of the devil, are you, Sera?

SERA: Pastor Al says to kill a child is to spit in God's eye.

SCOTT: What does that even mean?

SERA: Pastor Al says, "Whosoever sheds man's blood should his blood be shed; for man was made in God's image."

SCOTT: *(Smirking.)* Sounds like Pastor Al is in favour of the death penalty.

SERA: If that's what you heard, then you're not listening. I'm telling you, if you came to church with me just once, his words would inspire you.

SCOTT: To be more judgmental?

SERA: How am I being judgmental?

SCOTT: You support a man who advocates murder!

SERA: That's not what I'm doing and you're twisting my words. You always hear what you –

SCOTT: Always?

SERA: This is why I talk to him.

SCOTT: By him do you mean that Him *(Pointing up.)* or Pastor Al? Is that even his real name?

SERA: Why are you attacking my pastor?

SCOTT: Oh, come on Sera. I'm not attacking him, I'm just having some fun with you. It's "Pastor Al said this" and "Pastor Al said that," if I didn't know better I'd be jealous.

SERA: Don't be ridiculous.

SCOTT: Why? Because it sounds like you talk to him more than you talk to me.

SERA: There are things I can talk to him that I can't talk to you about.

SCOTT: If you have to go outside our marriage to talk to someone about anything, then that's a problem.

SERA: Faith, Scott. I can talk to him about my faith, my doubts and…and…and the fact that my beliefs are slipping.

SCOTT: Doubts are healthy, Sera.

SERA: See, this is what I'm talking about, you don't understand because to you religion is a joke.

SCOTT: I never said that.

SERA: You don't understand, you don't understand, you don't understand!!

SCOTT: Then help me!

SERA: I can't. I'm a Christian doubting my faith in everything that used to seem so certain. You as a non-believer cannot help me. The only thing keeping me afloat is the one thing you think it's okay to mock, so of course I turn to my pastor when I need someone to talk to.

SCOTT: I can listen. Isn't that enough? Do you have to go to your pastor with every crisis without talking to me first?

*SERA walks out of the room and returns with the pregnancy test.*

SERA: Why did you save this?

SCOTT: Why didn't you throw it away?

*SERA throws the test at him.*

SERA: Don't turn this back on me! I'm not the only one holding onto invisible things.

SCOTT: What the fuck does that mean? And where is this anger coming from right now?

SERA: I wish we could start over. I don't want to be stuck in this grief that lives in this house. I want to be released from feeling like a walking tomb. *(Long pause.)* When we got married I was sure that I wanted kids. Convinced. But the longer we were married the more I enjoyed…us. I have so many friends with kids, some who got married long after us and are already on their second or third. I've been to too many baby showers and toddlers' birthday parties where they're celebrated like they're going to Yale. I am sick of looking at friends' Facebook pages that show no evidence of who they are because their children now represent them. I like us. I liked our life before *(She picks up the test.)* this was the finish line.

SCOTT: Is this because of what happened at the dinner party?

SERA: You're not listening.

SCOTT: You're not making any sense.

SERA: Honestly? I put off having kids and gave you every excuse to avoid getting pregnant, but eventually I gave in.

SCOTT: You can be such a martyr! We decided a long time ago that we wanted kids.

SERA: We did, but then I changed my mind.

SCOTT: Before or after you got pregnant, because… if you stopped wanting kids after the first miscarriage then –

SERA: You'd understand? Then you could understand? You couldn't understand if I just didn't feel the desire, the urge to be a parent?

SCOTT: No, I mean, yes, but…five times? We've been –

SERA: We?

SCOTT: I was there too, Sera.

SERA: You want to know how I feel? You say that I don't tell you how I'm feeling…well, it's because the things I feel and think are rotten, stinking, and hateful. I hate my body and I hate myself. I look in the mirror and see an enemy. My body is my enemy. My knees are raw and ashy from praying. I pray in the bathroom after you go to bed because I know how uncomfortable it makes you. The tiles are cold and they remind me that being a supplicant isn't supposed to feel good. Seeing my hands in prayer makes feel like a beggar, a beggar asking for something that other women take for granted. My hormones make me feel unstable and crazy; I yell at the kids in my class for stupid things and resent them because they exist.

SCOTT: It's natural to feel resentful against children when you've had so much trouble.

SERA: You're not hearing me! I feel like a – a way-station for children to die. Instead of being filled with God's light and forgiveness, I am angry. I'm angry all the time, and the only place I can get release is by talking to my pastor.

SCOTT: Why, why would you go through all that if you didn't want a baby?

SERA: I want to stay married.

SCOTT: We'd never get divorced over this.

SERA: Marriages have ended on less.

SCOTT: We're not Rushton and Anaar. We've been together since we were seventeen! I thought I knew how you felt about everything.

SERA: I don't want to keep trying. For children, I just can't. I'm losing my faith, Scott, and barely had a hold of it when we started trying to get pregnant. I remember telling my friends that you being in my life was proof that God exists. And they would say the real proof of His love is a child. They said looking at your first child is like seeing the face of God. I wanted to want the desire to be a mother but I felt nothing. I prayed for the want and got silence. The first pregnancy was an accident. I didn't want it. My more devout friends said it was God's gift, that He must have believed that we were ready. So when I miscarried it was a relief, but you were so upset. You've always wanted kids more than I did. At that time I still thought I was just slow to warm to the idea and that it was always the wrong time, at least that's how it felt.

SCOTT: I need you to get off your knees and look at me instead of your God for whatever it is you want.

SERA: See, no. No, that's not how this works, Scott. I feel like you're asking me to make a choice. I wanted to have a baby for us, but I didn't want a baby. I prayed and every time I got pregnant it was taken away so… obviously God has spoken. If a child is a gift, proof of His love, then what do the miscarriages mean? If I lose my faith in Him, then what do I have?

SCOTT: You have me.

SERA: The Lord giveth and the Lord taketh away. Do you see –

SCOTT: No, I don't.

SERA: If asked to make a choice between my faith and you, then –

SCOTT: Why does there have to be a choice? Why would there ever be a choice? I'm here, right here, and you're grasping at-at-at…smoke, vapours, while praying for what? A baby? Not to have a baby? How do you hold two contrasting desires in your mind and not get lost?

SERA: I think we need to step back, think about what we want and figure this out.

SCOTT: Figure this out? We haven't decided anything! You need God more than me, right? I'm here and he's left you. How are *we* supposed to fix this? You need to fix your attitude towards me and how your religion is shutting me out.

SERA: It's not my religion and you've always been free to come to church with me.

SCOTT: Not gonna happen.

SERA: It's lonely going to church alone. I need you beside me.

SCOTT: I'm an atheist and I hate the way your faith makes you blame everything on yourself when things don't go your way. I wanted kids with you, but if you don't want them, then we'll be fine. This isn't your fault or mine and it certainly has nothing to do with God.

SERA: If you ask me to choose between you and my God, then you can't win. Without my faith I'm nothing.

SCOTT: Jesus!

SERA: Come to church with me.

SCOTT: No.

*SCOTT walks back to the groceries and continues to unpack them. There is a very long silence.*

SERA: You didn't answer my question.

SCOTT: Which one?

SERA: Why did you keep the test?

SCOTT: The test…the test…mm, yes, well…I'm not like you, Sera. Or maybe I am. I don't know, I just wanted to hold onto the proof that this one, this baby, Ava, was really here, or almost here. I understand that you put more energy into a book that helps you do the heavy lifting when our relationship gets hard. I can't do that. I'm sorry, but I really believe that religion makes otherwise moral people do stupid things.

SERA: You're judging me?

SCOTT: If not me, then who? I respect you, I don't respect the shield of religion you throw up every time things go sideways. We cannot control everything we want or don't want with a prayer. Maybe we can't have children because…we just can't, and not because you're being punished or taught a lesson. Don't turn this into being about my beliefs or lack of them, because then you're just changing the subject again so we don't have to deal with the loss.

SERA: Do not be yoked together with unbelievers. For what do righteousness and wickedness have in common?

SCOTT: Enough with the scripture.

SERA: Pastor Al says –

SCOTT: You know what? Maybe Pastor Al should be here to fuck you since I obviously can't give you what you want.

SERA: *(Pause. Then, very quietly.)* How do you know he hasn't?

SCOTT: What?

SERA: I bought condoms.

SCOTT: What?!

SERA: It was just once. I thought that maybe it was you that was broken, not me.

SCOTT: I don't believe you. This is your hormones making you behave this way. You haven't been yourself for a long time now and I shouldn't have pushed you to have that dinner.

SERA: You don't believe me.

SCOTT: You would never cheat on me. Remember in high school when I was leaving for university and you said, "You and me are swans, and swans mate for life." You were right. This is us.

SERA: That's right. So, tell me the truth, are you sad that you won't be a father?

SCOTT: *(Pause.)* No. As long as I have you, I'll be okay.

SERA: I believe you.

*Long pause they stare at each other until SCOTT folds and sits at the table.*

SCOTT: I, uh…well, I don't see any point in telling you this now, but –

SERA: *(Quietly.)* I cheated?

SCOTT: What?

SERA: You were saying…

SCOTT: Yeah, I had a little problem at work…the presentation…the one I killed myself over? Yeah. Didn't go so well.

SERA: Oh.

SCOTT: I lost some big accounts.

SERA: Ah.

SCOTT: Yes. But… it's been weighing on me…. I'm going to have to start looking for another job. I know I should have told you right away, but I was feeling like such a coward….I'm coming clean now. I'm sorry.

SERA: Okay.

*She looks at him expecting a confession. Long pause.*

Oh… I thought you were…going to say – something else.

SCOTT: I feel good now that I can say my conscience is clear. You're not angry?

SERA: I'm tired. I'm very, very tired. I think I'll lie down for a bit.

SCOTT: Want some company?

SERA: No, no…thanks though. *(She starts to leave.)*

SCOTT: Blessed be the poor in spirit for theirs is the kingdom of Heaven.

SERA: *(Turning back.)* What?

SCOTT: It's the only thing I remember from Sunday school. Matthew 5:3, right? My birthday is on May 3 and my middle name is Matthew, so I always remembered that proverb.

*SERA walks over, strokes SCOTT's face.*

SERA: Right. You know, some days I wish I could be reborn.

SCOTT: Go for your nap and you will be. I promise.

*SERA kisses him and exits. SCOTT goes back to unpacking the groceries. He eventually pulls out a box of condoms, looks in the direction that SERA has left.*

*SCOTT and SERA's bedroom. She is on her knees, beside the bed in prayer. The lights are dim, she is in spotlight and SCOTT is watching her in the background.*

SERA: God grant me the serenity to accept the things I cannot change; the courage to change the things I can; and the wisdom to know the difference. Living one day at a time; enjoying one moment at a time. Accepting hardships as the pathway to peace. Taking, as He did, this sinful world as it is, not as I would have it. Trusting that He will make all things right if I surrender to His Will, that I may be reasonably happy in this life and supremely happy with Him forever in the next. Amen.

*The sound of birdsong (chimney swallow/ common chaffinch/ wrens) grows in volume as the lights fade to black.*

*The end.*